A SOLDIER'S LETTERS FROM VIETNAM

To: GENE
Thank you.

Compiled by Jeff Freppon

Printed in the United States of America
Published by Braughler Books LLC., Springboro, Ohio

First printing, 2020

ISBN: 978-1-970063-64-6

Library of Congress Control Number: 2020909332

Ordering information: Special discounts are available on quantity
purchases by bookstores, corporations, associations, and others. For
details, contact the publisher at:

    sales@braughlerbooks.com
    or at 937-58-BOOKS

For questions or comments about this book, please write to:
    info@braughlerbooks.com

Braughler™
Books
braughlerbooks.com

Contents

ACKNOWLEDGEMENTS

First Division Museum Colonel Robert R. McCormick
Research Center Digital Collection
(https://firstdivisionmuseum.nmtvault.com)

Colonel Todd Mayer

Jerri White

Jim Freppon

Judy Smetana

Cecelia Freppon

David Braughler and the team at Braughler Books

Dedicated to Jack

INTRODUCTION

John Dennis Freppon (Jack Jr.), my older brother, was the 1st born of a set of twins on August 12, 1948 in Cincinnati, Ohio. His sister Geraldine (Jerri) was born minutes later. He weighed 6 pounds and 3 ounces.

I am almost 11 years younger than the twins, so my childhood memories of both are vague and somewhat blurry. Jack didn't talk much about what he did in Vietnam, but I do have a somewhat vivid memory of horse playing with him when he was home on leave and he described taking long underwear off a dead soldier and wearing them because he was cold.

Jack and Jerri were constant companions, played baseball with their friends and attended school together until secondary classes began, when Jack went to Purcell High and Jerri went to Marian High. Jack was rather independent and challenged authority frequently, especially during his parochial education. "Bullheaded" and "stubborn" are terms I heard describing him. Jack tested educational boundaries since he believed he could design better curricula suited to his interests and goals, so he wasn't the best traditional student but apparently he did well enough to be considered for university studies.

Both Jack and Jerri graduated in the Spring of 1966 and enrolled at the University of Cincinnati for fall Semester. Jerri committed to her college courses, but Jack felt he should be admitted into advanced political science and other courses without completing college English and other basic prerequisites. Jack got frustrated, changed direction, and decided he wanted to serve his country and enlisted in the Army for 36 months sometime during the semester.

Our father and mother were livid when they learned about Jack's Army enlistment. They hoped university study interested Jack and realized college attendance provided a draft deferment. They were proud their children were in college and would be the first to get advanced degrees in our family. Our father served in the military and knew the potential challenges and perils Jack would encounter. Both parents saw the terrible news about the Vietnam war as it was delivered nightly on the television and feared their oldest son would be sent into that meat grinder. I remember our parents' tears and sadness when Jack left but imagine he, even though torn by their grief, was excited about the grand adventure he was about to experience.

Looking back, I guess I am surprised that Jack volunteered to serve in such a command- centered organization like the Army. Jack challenged authority constantly. He did not want to sit in the barber's chair to get his hair cut. He confronted elementary school teachers who did not do enough to protect his twin sister from bullying. He defied high school and seminary educators who tried to control his direction. He constantly tested our parents who tried to guide him in their right direction. I envied his independence and am glad he was my brother.

Jack was assigned basic training at Fort Knox beginning on December 30, 1966. He graduated from basic training on March 3, 1967. He was assigned to AIT (Advanced Individual Training), enrolled in Journalism School in Colorado, then toured and wrote about his western U.S. experiences. He spent a week jungle training in Panama then was stationed at Fort Polk, Louisiana for his final 2 weeks of jungle training for Vietnam.

After AIT graduation, Jack went home to Cincinnati for 15 days then left for Fort Lewis, Washington where he was attached to the Airmobile Cavalry Intelligence and Security unit. He was there approximately 2 months then left for Vietnam.

Enroute to Vietnam, his ship stopped in Hawaii, Guam and Manila in the Philippines. He wrote and edited an Army newspaper during his voyage.

He arrived in Vietnam at age 18, for his first 12-month tour as an Army Private First Class in mid-July 1967.

I sincerely thank the First Division Museum Colonel Robert R. McCormick Research Center Digital Collection (https://firstdivisionmuseum.nmtvault.com) for providing access to extensive, detailed histories, stories of amazing heroism, issues of the American Traveler (newspaper for the 1st Infantry Division in Vietnam) and Danger Forward (chronicled battles, operations and other Army activities in Vietnam).

Jack served valiantly in Vietnam as an Infantry Operations and Intelligence Specialist in Company E, 1st Battalion, 18th Infantry, becoming a platoon squad leader and Staff Sergeant because of his ambition.

The heart of each chapter of the book is the collection of Jack's letters. There are 41 letters, 40 addressed to my parents and 1 addressed to Jerri, his fraternal twin. I transcribed each letter. Many are undated so I tried to put them in approximate chronological order. Some indicated where he was in Vietnam and contain graphic descriptions of what happened during his time there. They portrayed his experiences, feelings, and actions beginning during basic training.

Chapters are roughly arranged chronologically. I included battle histories and letters from comrades. Jerri (Jack's fraternal twin) and I traveled to Vietnam a few years ago and visited the Lai Khe area, where Jack spent a fair amount of time living and fighting in the country. Evidence of the American Army base remained, and we walked through the rubber plantation and photographed bunkers that are slowly disappearing in the jungle. Those pictures are on the last few pages.

This book attempts to honor Jack and others who served in Vietnam. All proceeds from book sales go to the John (Jack) D. Freppon Scholarship Fund at Purcell-Marian High School.

Additional donations can be sent to:

Purcell-Marian High School
John (Jack) D. Freppon
Scholarship Fund
2935 Hackberry Street
Cincinnati, Ohio 45206

CHAPTER ONE

ARMY TRAINING

A little over 50 years have passed since my older brother, Jack, served and fought in Vietnam.

Jack was the sort of guy everyone counted on, someone who cared about others and showed it. I don't remember him being interested in guns or pretending to be in battles like I was as a youngster. I vaguely recall him being most interested in playing baseball until past dark in the street with friends. When the streetlights came on, I recollect him tossing his ball glove up toward the light and watching bats swoop and dance around the raggedy leather shape which seemed to take forever to fall.

In this Chapter, I share the letters he wrote during training, prior to leaving for Vietnam. Before Jack went to fight, he endured and passed Basic and Advanced Individual Army training. Information about what he learned is presented and you can see his doodling on the back of a pamphlet describing 'Things Soldiers Should Know', indicated some level of creativity especially since our father and Jack's twin are artists.

Jack was glad to graduate from Basic Training and he enjoyed his experiences at Army Journalism school in Colorado while seeing much in western states. He wrote about discontentment among his comrades during jungle training and knew he would be going to the front line in Vietnam but felt it was useless to worry about it. I think Jack, like anyone going to war, was concerned about his upcoming journey but probably excited and confident about his fighting skills. He endured and successfully completed tough training. He was worried about what was going on at home but never seemed homesick or depressed but rather enjoyed his new opportunities and adventures.

He was focused on his pay, his chances of getting shot and what he would be doing after his time in Vietnam. Those themes repeat in future letters and evolve as Jack becomes an experienced fighter.

ORGANIZATION OF US ARMY UNITS

FIELD ARMY	50,000 + SOLDIERS	COMMANDED BY 4 STAR GENERAL
CORPS	2-5 DIVISIONS 20-45,000 SOLDIERS	COMMANDED BY 3 STAR LT. GENERAL
DIVISION	3 BRIGADES 10-15,000 SOLDIERS	COMMANDED BY 2 STAR MAJOR GENERAL
BRIGADE OR GROUP/ REGIMENT	2-5 BATTALIONS 3-5,000 SOLDIERS	COMMANDED BY 1 STAR BRIGADIER GENERAL OR COLONEL
BATTALION OR SQUADRON	4-6 COMPANIES 300-1,000 SOLDIERS	COMMANDED BY LIEUTENANT COLONEL

COMPANY OR BATTERY/ TROOP	3-5 PLATOONS 62-190 SOLDIERS	COMMANDED BY CAPTAIN OR FIRST LIEUTENANT OR MAJOR
PLATOON	2-4 SQUADS 16-44 SOLDIERS	COMMANDED BY SECOND LIEUTENANT
SQUAD/ SECTION	9-10 SOLDIERS	COMMANDED BY SERGEANT

MILITARY ACRONYMS

ACAV	ARMED CAVALRY ASSAULT VEHICLES
ARTY	ARTILLERY
ARVN	ARMY OF THE REPUBLIC OF VIETNAM
BN	BATTALION
CIDG	CIVILIAN IRREGULAR DEFENSIVE GROUP
CP	COMMAND POST
DTOC	DIVISION TACTICAL OPERATIONS CENTER
DMZ	DEMILITARIZED ZONE
EOD	EXPLOSIVE ORDNANCE DISPOSAL
FSB	FIRE SUPPORT BASE
FSPB	FIRE SUPPORT PATROL BASE
GI	GROUND INFANTRYMAN
KIA	KILLED IN ACTION
LCT	LAND CLEARING TEAM
LOH	LIGHT OBSERVATION HELICOPTER
LP	LISTENING POST
LZ	LANDING ZONE
MACV	MILITARY ASSISTANCE COMMAND CENTER
MEDCAP	MEDICAL CIVIL ACTION PROGRAM
NDP	NIGHT DEFENSIVE POSITION
NVA	NORTH VIETNAMESE ARMY
OPCON	OPERATIONAL CONTROL
PSYOPS	PSYCHOLOGICAL OPERATIONS
PZ	PICKUP ZONE
RIF	RECONNAISSANCE-IN-FORCE
RON	REST OVERNIGHT
RPG	ROCKET PROPELLED GRENADE
R&R	REST AND RECUPERATION (RELAXATION)
RRF	RAPID REACTION FORCE
TAOI	TACTICAL AREA OF INTEREST
VC	VIET CONG

JACK'S US ARMY JOURNEY BEGINS AT FORT KNOX, KENTUCKY DECEMBER 30, 1966

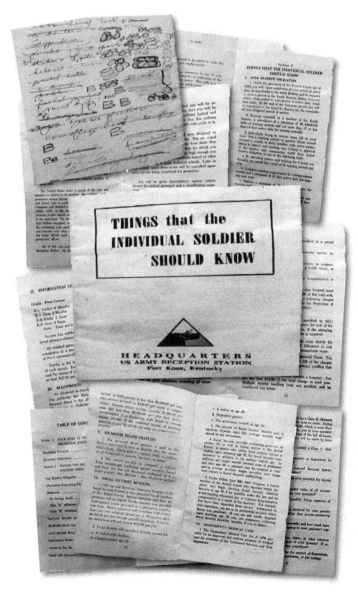

BASIC COMBAT TRAINING

THE FIRST STEPS TO BECOMING A SOLDIER

Basic Combat Training, often known as "boot camp", is the introduction to Army service, where recruits learn the traditions, tactics and methods of becoming a Soldier.

During Basic, recruits learn how to work as a member of a team to accomplish tasks. They learn discipline, including proper dress, marching, and grooming standards. Most importantly, they are instilled with the Seven Core Army Values and the Soldier Creed.

Basic Combat Training comes in three phases and lasts about ten weeks, depending on a selected military occupational specialty (MOS). After graduating from basic training, recruits undergo two additional phases of training, known as Advanced Individual Training, where they learn the job skills required of the MOS.

RED PHASE: DISCIPLINE, VALUES, TEAMWORK

This is the first true phase of becoming a Soldier and adapting to life in the Army. During this phase, recruits receive general orientation, army uniform, and an army-issued haircut.

Recruits learn how to comport themselves as Soldiers and are expected to recite the Warrior Ethos and Soldier's Creed. They receive briefings on basic first aid and sexual harassment and sexual assault awareness and prevention programs.

This phase also includes physical readiness training, road marches, confidence building, and formation marching. They receive an introduction into Chemical Radioactive Biological and Nuclear (CBRN) readiness, which will include the proper usage of breathing masks. At the end of this phase, recruits receive an Army Unit Patch to be worn on the left shoulder of their uniforms.

WHITE PHASE: LEARNING THE BASIC SKILLS OF A SOLDIER

Welcome to the rifle range. During this phase of Basic, recruits begin training their assigned primary weapon, learning the basics of rifle marksmanship, maintenance, and engaging targets at varying distances. During this phase, they also learn hand-to-hand training and how to prioritize multiple targets simultaneously.

In addition to marksmanship training, they also continue physical fitness training, and are expected to navigate obstacle courses and rappel from a 50-foot structure, known as the Warrior Tower.

White phase will also be the first introduction to Warrior Tasks and Battle Drills.

BLUE PHASE: OVERCOMING FINAL CHALLENGES

The final phase of Basic Combat Training builds on everything recruits have learned so far and will serve as the final rite of passage from civilian to Soldier.

During this phase, they continue learning advanced marksmanship and maneuvering techniques, including engaging targets as part of a team, convoy operations, and identifying and disabling improvised explosive devices. They train on advanced weapons, like machine guns and learn how to throw live grenades.

As part of their final challenges, they embark on a multiple-day land navigation course to test survival, fitness, and Soldier skills.

At the end of the phase, and after having passed all their challenges, recruits will be qualified to wear the Army Black Beret as a fully qualified Army Soldier.

WHAT RECRUITS LEARN DURING BASIC WARRIOR TASKS AND BATTLE DRILLS

During Basic Combat Training, recruits are introduced to the various tactical proficiencies they will be required to retain as a Soldier. These are called Warrior Tasks and Battle Drills and will serve as a foundation of Soldier skills. Warrior Tasks come in four forms, and involve mastering individual Soldier skills, while Battle Drills are team-based tactical skills.

SHOOT

This Warrior Task requires becoming qualified and proficient on their assigned weapon, which is determined through their chosen Military Occupational Specialty (MOS). Recruits learn how to properly engage targets, maintaining their weapon, and using periphery technology, including night vision and laser sighting.

Recruits will also be required to engage targets using the Army's array of machine guns. Finally, they must safely and accurately throw live hand grenades and set and recover mines.

MOVE

As a Soldier, movement relates to the ability to determine location on the ground and navigate from one point to another while avoiding obstacles. This skill also requires knowing how to properly prepare a vehicle for a convoy.

COMMUNICATE

In a combat situation, communication is crucial, both verbally and non-verbally. With this Warrior Task, recruits must be able to execute a situation report, known as a "sitrep", call for fire support at the proper coordinates, and order a medevac. They must also know proper hand signaling during low profile operations.

SURVIVE

The survival skill relates to the ability to deal with danger situations. Recruits must know how to move and react to direct and indirect fire, engage in hand-to-hand combat, disarm and avoid explosive devices, and perform first aid

BATTLE DRILLS

Battle Drills are team-based exercises that hone abilities to work with the other members of a unit. Some battle drills include:

- Reacting to enemy contact

- Dismounting a vehicle during combat

- Evacuating injured personnel during combat

- Dealing with chemical and biological attacks

GRADUATION

If recruits advance past the final phase of Basic, they will be eligible to wear the Black Beret as a full Army Soldier.

As part of the final requirements, recruits must be able to demonstrate the following:

FINAL REQUIREMENTS TO PASS
BASIC COMBAT TRAINING

- Complete an Army Physical Fitness Test (APFT), scoring at least 50 points in each event.
- Safely handle and maintain their primary assigned weapon

Jack shooting his rifle

- Pass the chemical training confidence exercises, demonstrating the ability to properly use a protective mask
- Demonstrate proficiency in all Warrior Tasks and Battle Drills
- Demonstrate proficiency in First Aid
- Negotiate the obstacle course
- Complete hand-to-hand combat (combative) training
- Pass the hand grenade qualification course
- Complete a 16K tactical foot march
- Pass a small-team land navigation course
- Complete any other tactical field training or situation training exercises[1]

Jack's Army graduation photograph

February 1967

Dear Mom and Dad,

We just had our PT test and I passed it. It was raining and it was cold. We crawled through the mud and we were so wet and cold we didn't care what we did. Well we only have 2 more weeks to go. All we have left major-wise is the night bivouac (sleeping out) which is Thursday and the C-41 test which we must take to graduate. The good thing is this week is George Washington's birthday so we can have a day off. We also begin tossing live hand-grenades Friday and that should be interesting. They still haven't talked to me about my orders for AIT (After Basic Training) but I have an appointment to talk to the Company Commander.

We just got our medals for rifle marksmanship and they are sharp. Now we turn those in, and we're finished with them. Saturday, we had our Inspector General inspection and if that wasn't strict. The General of the base picked two companies, one of them us and he came through and inspected each man individually. We had to dress up in our formal green uniform and lay out our footlockers, our display rack, and our bunk. Our platoon came out second and I think we're going to be an honor company. I'm writing this letter while I'm supposed to be working as barracks orderly. I'm supposed to straighten up the barracks and watch out, so no one steals anything. Some guy in our barracks got caught sleeping on fireguard and got an Article 15 but instead of taking it he tries to kill himself with an overdose of drugs. He almost died but they saved him and that kid I told you about, you know the one who deserted, well they gave him 4 years at hard labor. We send in our laundry for the last time this week, so time is drawing near to leave. I think I can get a pass this weekend, so I'll call you Friday night and clear you up on this. We have to get shots tomorrow. I think they're only cold shots to prevent the flu.

About 2 weeks ago we were on a march and we were supposed to be tear-gassed from an airplane. We marched down the road and suddenly, a plane came out of nowhere and dropped tear gas. We put on the gas mask and waited for a second and then those asses made us take those masks off and that tear gas burned your eyes and made you cough so that you had to stop. We also went out on the Infiltration Course the night it snowed 5 inches. Talking about cold and wet. I was so cold that night I honestly asked God to take me from this Earth. It scares the living daylights out of me when those machine guns started firing and those dynamite charges started going off. There was only one guy hurt. He got scared and stood up. He was wounded twice in the shoulder. They had tracers in between the live ammo and these light up the area which was quite a sight. We crawled under barbed wire and in and out of trenches.

We should be graduating March 3rd and should leave March 4th or 5th. If I don't get a leave, I don't think I'll be home for another 6 months if they send me to Colorado or Oklahoma but I'm pretty sure I'll get a pass this weekend if all goes well. Things are looking up now. They're giving us more time to eat, better food, and more than scraps to eat. The harassment is almost gone, and we're being treated right now. We get this over with and they say AIT is fun compared to Basic Training. So, I can't wait to get out of here. If Bill is considering coming in here, tell him to forget it because the heavier you are the rougher, they are on you. They would crucify him on a PT stand. Well tell everyone I say hello. I better get going.

Love,

Jack

ADVANCED INDIVIDUAL TRAINING

Learning an Army Military Occupational Specialty (MOS)

After completing Basic Combat Training, recruits are ready for the next step. Advanced Individual Training (AIT) is where they will learn the skills to perform their Army job.

At one of many diverse AIT schools, they receive hands-on training and field instruction to make them an expert in that specific career field. They also gain the discipline and work ethic to help them no matter what path they take in life.[2]

FORT POLK

There were two simulated Vietnamese hamlets that featured earthen berms, sharpened bamboo stake defenses, and booby-trap simulations. The largest village was Tiger Land covering between three and four acres.

Tiger Land was complete with a schoolhouse, shrines and farm animals as well as bamboo stake defenses, booby traps and tunnels. Everything a Soldier might encounter in and around a Vietnamese village was incorporated.

Trainees would search the village for weapons caches and interview the villagers to determine whether they supported the North Vietnamese.

Bunkers and perimeter foxholes would be manned throughout the night regardless of weather conditions. During the night enemy role players would make some type of probe on the defensive lines around the village.

Instructors observed everything recruits did. If the trainees did something wrong or something could be done better, the instructors explained it. Questioning the villagers, finding and defusing booby traps, finding the best fields of fire, and maintaining their weapons and equipment were things instructors would focus on.

By 1969, Fort Polk had dispatched more soldiers to Vietnam than any other military post in the nation.[3]

May 1, 1967

Dear Mom and Dad,

Since I left Fort Knox, I've been in almost every state west of the Mississippi. I've hardly had time to write.

I was at Colorado Springs 4 weeks at Journalism school, then to California for a week, then just on a tour of the west and writing about it. It's been great. The west is beautiful. The Rocky Mountains are huge. I never saw anything like them.

Then just last week they sent a jet load of us to Panama to spend a week in the jungle. This was terrible. I'll tell you more about it when I get home. Now I'm here in Louisiana taking my final 2 weeks of jungle training for Vietnam.

We got our orders to report to Washington to be connected with the newly forming Second Air Mobile Cavalry Unit. It is just forming so it will be a few months before I go over probably. After these next 2 weeks are over, I'll be coming home for a month. So, get ready.

A group of us are going to New Orleans today for 2 days.

Fort Polk is the most desolate place in the south. There is nothing here except every poisonous snake and every kind of spider imaginable. I hate it here. They even have a life-size Viet Cong village where they train soldiers. There are only people training for Vietnam down here and there's a feeling of discontentment in the air. It's hard to explain.

But like I said before I will be home in 2 weeks. Look for me around on a Saturday because I'm going to catch a jet home and we're through with training on that Friday.

How's things going? Did you sell the house? Did Jerri get her scholarship renewed? How are the kids doing? Tell John the west is the only place to go. It's beautiful beyond all description. I didn't have much time out there but what I saw and did do, I enjoyed immensely. The most beautiful state is Colorado, then California, and then Arizona. There was so much to see and do but my time was limited.

I will be going to Vietnam after my leave and from the training they gave us it will be a little risky. I will be on the front line most of the time reporting for different situations and actions. Some of the guys are really homesick and some are scared about going to Vietnam, but I tell them it's life and there's no use in worrying about it. If you're meant to go over, you must go over and if it's your time to go, it's your time to go. So, I must be going, and I will see you in 2 weeks.

Your son,

Jack

Spring 1967

Dear Mom and Dad,

I received your letters and it was good to hear from you. I am delighted that you sold the house and wait until I see the new one. I'll be home sometime Saturday morning. My jet leaves New Orleans at 4:00 Friday so I'll call when it gets to Greater Cincinnati Airport. The circumstances covering my funds are good. I have $250 saved up so there's no concern about that problem. I'll be home only 15 days before going to Fort Lewis, Washington. I am attached to the Intelligence and Security branch of the newly formed unit of the First (Airmobile) Cavalry.

It is a tough unit but a good one but with a little luck I'll be in Washington (State) maybe for a few months so they are in no hurry to send me over and when I do go, it will take a month to get there on a ship (and get this, the ship stops in Hawaii for a few days). I hope Jerri gets her scholarship even though we're out of the city. Do you think she'll get it? How's the kids doing? I guess Dad's happy to be closer to work. I'm glad we're moving. It'll be a year and a half before I can even come home for a visit. I'll be in Vietnam for 11 months and off and on the front lines, but I don't think I'll have any problems and if I do get shot there's less than 1% who die from their wounds.

I'm fixing to get a Class Q allotment and increase my bond to $25 a month. I plan to send 2/3 of my money home every month and when I get to Vietnam I'll get overseas pay, combat and hazardous duty pay. I'll be making around $350 a month and send around $300 a month home so it won't stay over there. After 12 months this money plus my bonds will accumulate. I'll talk to you more about this when I get home. So, don't worry. I'll be in Greater Cincinnati

Airport around 9:00 Saturday morning but don't come until I call you so I must be going now. See you Saturday. Say hello to everyone.

Jack

P.S. Please don't tell Bill I'll come over and see him. I want to surprise him. You don't write because I'll probably be gone before I receive it. See you Saturday.

CHAPTER TWO
EARLY-SUMMER 1967

JOURNEY AND ARRIVAL IN VIETNAM

I estimated that Jack left the US on his sea journey aboard the USS Geiger in late June or early July.

His fourth letter described his ship experience and what he anticipated. Our family didn't travel much before Jack went to Vietnam. We visited the local amusement park yearly but undoubtedly Jack was curious about the world as he got older. Enlisting in the Army provided opportunities to travel and experience a different life. Jack saw new and unusual sights while onboard. He met a Marine on the ship who had been stationed in Vietnam and learned a bit about what he will face. He mused about taking an around-the-world sea voy-

age and writing a book about his Vietnam experiences after getting out of the Army.

Jack arrived in Vietnam in mid-July 1967 and he indicated he liked being there. He was learning about the Vietnamese people and getting accustomed to the climate and living conditions. Almost every letter included questions about what was happening at home. He asks about my face, which apparently was damaged trying to catch a baseball, but I do not recall getting hurt. I remember looking up to him as some sort of mythical deity but mistakenly assumed my existence meant little because of our age difference. He cared about everyone he knew.

Jack indicated a willingness to serve longer if necessary, wanted to learn Vietnamese and realized he may die fighting. He proudly wrote that his First Army Division (Big Red One) unit was nicknamed the 'Swamp Rats' and he wore a black beret. I recall Jack almost always wearing a baseball cap and wondered if he slept wearing it, so I understand why he liked his new hat.

His pay and potential earnings are a constant theme. He always had a job as a teen and wanted to earn and spend his own money. He understood and valued personal responsibility. His letters indicated a desire for additional duties leading to higher rank and income.

I include maps outlining unit assignments in Vietnam, and a couple Jack sent home with comments regarding his location in the country. I vaguely remember seeing a world globe in his room so geography must have been one of his interests. He frequently commented about his location and potential placement in most of his letters.

Jack shared somewhat positive impressions about his new home and neighbors, but these opinions will change as he starts to experience battle action.

USS GEIGER

USS Geiger photographs

July 1967

Dear Mom and Dad,

Well by the time you'll receive this, I'll be in Vietnam. We are in Guam (a small island) refueling and getting resupplied in food and water. We have been on the ocean for 25 days now and it was pretty tiresome. Most of the guys were seasick the first couple days but this wore off.

You have to see this ship to believe it. It's pretty small and there's 1500 men on it. It's so hot down in the sleeping quarters and we're so cramped it is difficult to breathe.

There are all sorts of weird sights out here in the ocean. We've seen whales, sharks, flying fish, and a few other commodities. The sea is beautiful, clear and blue. A constant breeze is our only relief from the heat. One boy jumped overboard, and we never found him. They think he went crazy and jumped.

The sunsets are unbelievable. You can't describe the beauty of the sea. After I get out, I would like to take a voyage around the world on a boat. We also had a boy almost die of appendicitis, but a boat came along side and took him off.

Did you receive my box of personal belongings? Everybody's just realizing the gravity of going to Vietnam. It didn't seem real while we were at Fort Lewis, but now, just thinking about it gives some guys the shakes. To me, I don't think it's going to be that bad. It's going to be different and, in a way, exciting. I am in no way afraid to face death if it comes to that. I am set with God and have peace of mind.

If it comes that I have to serve longer than one year in Vietnam, I'll do it, without too much to say. The money can't be beat and I'm going to put all the money I earn in the Soldiers Deposit, where it will draw 10% interest. Once I'm there I don't think it will be too bad. *The only thing I dislike is this intense heat. Everyone is literally "baked" from the sun already. I've even begun taking notes and writing to maybe publish a book, if anybody likes it, on my experience in Vietnam.*

Well I boo-booed again. They're not letting us mail letters for security reasons, but I tell you Guam is pretty but not much is here. I'm sending you a booklet telling you about the place.

We are now heading for the Philippine Islands. I will be in Manila for a day.

I had a real down-to-earth talk with a Marine and he told me some hints that will help me survive. One thing I am going to enjoy is R&R (a 5-day vacation) after I'm in Vietnam for 6 months. You can go to Thailand, Taiwan (Nationalist China), Japan, Hawaii or any other island in the Pacific. It is sort of a way to fight battle fatigue. I think I'll go to Japan because it is the most interesting place in the Orient.

Things are so cheap over here that you're going to have a nice Christmas this year. I'm not going to waste my money on women and whiskey like most of these fools. I'd rather spend it on the family than myself. Off-and-on you're going to get little packages of things which might be interesting.

One thing that Marine said was that it gets so hot here that you take the hottest day in the states and you double that, and you have the temperature in Vietnam. He said the filth and disease are your real enemies. He also said I will be stationed 20 miles outside Saigon with already made barracks and showers.

Well we're having rough seas. They said a small typhoon is coming. It's peculiar to see a storm from a distance. The clouds are low and black. The sea is calm then rough. A fog can be seen, and it slowly moves like a tiger, sneaking up on its' prey.

Tell Dad the Navy chow is twice as good as the Army. I am on the USS Geiger. The only complaint is that it is a little crowded. We have movies and snack bars and even a PX. Even with these, it is dirty and uncomfortable. There are no chairs for us to sit on, so we always sit on the floor. This is not so bad but 9/10ths of the time, it's dirty. An interesting fact is that this ship is 30 years-old and it's been sunk 3 times.

We have 2 submarines for escorts. They come up occasionally, and it's interesting to see them.

One thing on the sea, you're happy to see anything move on the water. Like a fish or whale but especially exciting is seeing a ship or vessel out a way but the real sight is to pass an island. You know the feeling of those early explorers when you see land.

We have a newspaper and I get a chance to write and edit. We get all the news (even sports scores). Those riots in the city finally quieted down, didn't they? Isn't all those strikes something?

We are a day ahead of you (International Dateline) but they said we should arrive in Vietnam Thursday.

Most everybody is broke (but I have a 5-dollar bill) and since I smoke my pipe, they can't bum cigarettes. I have 2 college grads who are my closest buddies, one graduated from Central Michigan State and majored in Psychology. The other graduated from Penn State and majored in engineering.

I'm bound and determined to learn the Vietnamese language. It will be useful when I go back to school and if I go through, I might use it to get into the State Department. I was talking to a Lieutenant and he said when I get back, the Army will send you to college. There's a deal like that since I'm RA (Regular Army) and with 18 months remaining after I get back from Vietnam, I'll go to some college or university.

But the only thing is, I'd like to spend a year in Germany or England, but if that college deal goes, screw Germany or England.

Then after I get out, the Army will pay you $125 a month for every month you served in the Army. So, since I'm in for 36 months, the Army will pay me $4000 (equivalent to 4 years college). They even help pay for your graduate work if you want it. Since they raised combat pay to $95 plus the $10 overseas pay and $120 will be my pay for the first 4-6 months while in Vietnam. I can speak a little

Vietnamese and I'm going to learn all I can about its' customs and language over there because it may come in handy if I apply to the State Department to get a job.

As a matter of fact, I'm looking forward to going over there and I'm not afraid to face the fact that I also may die there. Some of these guys are so afraid and lonesome that they are going AWOL and the only thing they'll get out of that is a jail sentence. More about that second time in Vietnam, I was talking to a Lieutenant and asked his advice. He said since I have 17 months left in the service after Vietnam, I stand a real good chance to get sent over there for another year. He told me to ask for an extension of 6 months (which could bring me home for Christmas) which would bring my months down to 11 and then ask for 10 months in Korea or Japan. This could get me out of serving another 6 months in Vietnam.

How's the new house? How are the neighbors? Did Jerri get her scholarship? Did Jeff pass? How does Dad like the house? Tell the kids I said hello and don't be surprised to find a box in the mail loaded with Vietnamese souvenirs. I'll look for some exotic Vietnamese clothes for everybody. How would you like a kimono? HA HA. Well I should be going. I've talked too much. Goodbye.

Love,
Jack

VOYAGE OF THE USS GEIGER TO VIETNAM

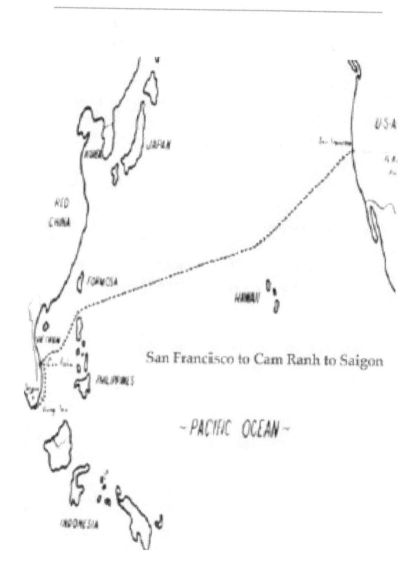

San Francisco to Cam Ranh to Saigon

RULES FOR SOLDIERS
IN VIETNAM

NINE RULES

For Personnel of U.S. Military
Assistance Command, Vietnam

The Vietnamese have paid a heavy price in suffering for their long fight against the Communists. We military men are in Vietnam now because their government has asked us to help its soldiers and people in winning their struggle. The Viet Cong will attempt to turn the Vietnamese people against you. You can defeat them at every turn by the strength, understanding, and generosity you display with the people. Here are the nine simple rules:

"Remember we are special guests here; we make no demands and seek no special treatment.

"Join with the people! Understand their life, use phrases from their language, and honor their customs and laws.

"Treat women with politeness and respect.

"Make personal friends among the soldiers and common people.

"Always give the Vietnamese the right of way.

"Be alert to security and ready to react with your military skill.

"Don't attract attention by loud, rude, or unusual behavior.

"Avoid separating yourself from the people by a display of wealth or privilege.

"Above all else you are members of the U.S. military forces on a difficult mission, responsible for all your official and personal actions. Reflect honor upon yourself and the United States of America."

"I'M RIGHT HERE":
VIETNAM MAPS JACK SENT HOME INDICATING HIS LOCATION AFTER ARRIVING IN THE COUNTRY IN JULY 1967

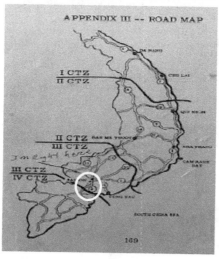

1st INFANTRY DIVISION HEADQUARTERS IN DI AN

July 26, 1967

Dear Mom and Dad,

We've been here almost a week and a half and it's not too bad. At this moment I am stationed at Di An. (pronounced Zion) 14 miles northeast of Saigon. We live in tents and all it does is rain. It is the monsoon season and it will be wet and muddy until December then the dry season will set in and it will be hot with a capital letter. The place where we live is a converted swamp and the mosquitos are in abundance. We have mosquito nets and spray we use. These jungle clothes they gave us are really good. They dry within an hour if they're soaking wet. My unit I'm attached with is the 1ˢᵗ Battalion of the 18ᵗʰ Division in the 1ˢᵗ Army Division. The nickname we have is the Swamp Rats. We wear black berets (hats like the Green Beret). It is a very good unit. There have only been 2 men killed in the last 9 months.

You should see these Vietnamese people. They are a curious lot. They always smile and bow but you can't really tell what they're thinking. You give them something and they act like you gave them the world. We had a little commotion the other day when we had a sniper (who was later killed) and a warning for a mortar bombing (which never came).

You might think this sounds crazy, but I really don't mind being over here, to be truthful, I like it. Since I'm in for the 3 years I won't mind it at all to spend another 6 months or a year over here. Then when I get back to the states, I can ask for a year in Germany because I don't want to be in the Army in the states. I hate teaching a bunch of guys who don't want to learn. What I really want to do is be a machine gunner on a helicopter, but I have to wait 3 months to do that. That will be another $60 a month plus I'll be a Sergeant fairly fast. Right now, I'm making $205 per month. After 2 or 3, I'll be promoted to Specialist-4 and then I'll make around $325-50 a month.

And if I stay longer, I'll be a Sergeant and make around $400 or $500 a month.

We have a barber shop run by the Vietnamese. For 40 cents you can get a haircut (which is as good, if not better than American barbers) then for another 10 cents you can get a massage and shampoo. You can get your clothes cleaned for 20 cents a set. We have a bar where you can get a shot of Canadian Club for 20 cents. Tape recorders, radios, cameras, watches, shavers and all other appliances can be bought for almost nothing. I'm sending you a Vietnamese 20 p (22 cents) and a 10 cent military script.

I got your letters and is Jeff's face all right? Tell him to keep practicing catching. Like I always said, Jeff can hit but catching needs

improvement. Tell Jim to get a glove with some of the money I sent home. Now if you ever get in any money problems don't be backward to use that money in the bank. I won't be needing it where I'm at. How is everybody? Please send me Bill's address and tell him to send me Paul's address. Also please send me Bob G.'s address.

Well I must go eat now so don't worry and I'll write again soon.

Love,

Jack

P.S. Tell everybody I said hello. Ask John if he wants a motorcycle. I might be able to send him one.

HISTORY OF THE BIG RED ONE

The First Infantry Division was authorized to be constituted in the Regular Army as Headquarters, First Expeditionary Division on 24 May 1917. It was officially organized under the command of Major General William L. Sibert on 8 June 1917. Comprised of veteran graduates of the US Military Academy and seasoned non-commissioned officers but consisting mainly of volunteers who had rushed to enlist after war was declared, the new division numbered 14,000 men—a figure which was to double by the cessation of hostilities.

The Division fought valiantly during World Wars 1 and 2. The Division suffered 22,320 casualties in World War 1 and boasted five Medal of Honor awards.

The Division suffered 21,023 casualties and had 16 Medals of Honor awarded during the Second World War. Following the war, the 1st Inf Div. remained in Germany as it did after the First World War. In the early summer of 1955, the BIG RED ONE returned to the United States after 13 years of continuous overseas duty. On 2 January 1964, it was reorganized under the ROAD concept.

Faced with increasing aggression from communist North Vietnam and widespread terrorist and guerrilla activities of the Viet Cong, the government of South Vietnam asked the Free World for assistance in the late 1950s. The United States responded by sending military advisors to work with the South Vietnamese armed forces. By 1965 the situation had reached the point where regular US units had to be summoned, if South Vietnam was not to be overrun by the communists.

On 12 July 1965, the 2nd Brigade of the BIG RED ONE landed at Cam Ranh Bay and Vung Tau, making it the first element of an Infantry division to arrive in Vietnam. By 1 November the entire division, under the command of Major General Jonathan O. Seaman, was operational.

By the end of 1965, the Division killed 960 Viet Cong. The Division killed 1447 enemy Viet Cong by the end of 1966.

On 8 January 1967, the 1st Infantry Division launched Operation CEDAR FALLS, a multi-division search and destroy mission in the infamous Iron Triangle, 30 miles north of Saigon. When the operation ended 18 days later, 389 Viet Cong had been killed, another 471 had turned themselves in through the Chieu Hoi (Open Arms) Program and 180 more had been captured, for the largest number of VC personnel lost up until that time in the Vietnamese III Corps Tactical Zone.

Next came Operation JUNCTION CITY and 52 continuous days of pounding enemy forces in War Zone C. Units either organic to or under the operational control of the BIG RED ONE killed 1,203 Viet Cong and North Vietnamese soldiers. The biggest single battle victory achieved by the Division since its arrival in Vietnam took place at Ap Gu, when the 1st Battalion, 26th Infantry, killed 609 in two days of fighting, 31 March-1 April.

Operation MANHATTAN began on 23 April and uncovered one of the largest weapons and ammunition caches of the war. A Hoi Chanh (former Viet Cong) led the 2nd Battalion, 18th Infantry, to the find, which included 350 weapons and 314,450 rounds of ammunition.

On 29 September 1967 the Division initiated Operation SHENANDOAH II, one of the most significant operations of the war. Inside the space of two weeks, BIG RED ONE units fought two violent battles with the 271st VC Regiment, costing the enemy 222 men.

By the end of October, the focal point of the operation became Loc Ninh, a little village situated on a rubber plantation 40 miles north of Lai Khe. Here, the Viet Cong were attempting to overrun the Special Forces/Civilian Irregular Defense Group (CIDG) compound.

When the operation ended on 19 November, BIG RED ONE units had accounted for 993 enemy killed.

Bu Dop, the site of another CIDG compound 87 miles north of Saigon near the Cambodian border, was the scene of December fighting, amounting to another 132-enemy killed. Before the year was out, Division troops fought two more major battles.

On 31 January 1968, during the Vietnamese celebration of the Lunar New Year (Tet), the Viet Cong launched a series of simultaneous ground and mortar attacks against South Vietnam's major cities and allied military installations. In response to the attacks, the Division was summoned to help secure Saigon's sprawling Tan Son Nhut Air Base. By 13 February, units of the BIG RED ONE had killed well over 1,000 Viet Cong and North Vietnamese soldiers.

On March 11, the First Infantry Division entered a multi-division operation called QUYET THANG (Resolve to Win), during which it accounted for 429 enemy dead. On 7 April 1968, the Division embarked on the largest operation of the Vietnam War, Operation Toan Thang (Certain Victory), which involved all allied troops throughout the III Corps Tactical Zone. One of the primary jobs of this two-part operation is to stop the infiltration of the enemy into the Saigon area. Phase I, which ended 31 May, resulted in 1,739 enemy killed. Phase II of Operation TOAN THANG began in June 1968.

During the early days of September 1968, Loc Ninh again became the focal point of BIG RED ONE operations. Hard fighting broke out on 11 September when a Special Forces compound was hit by a heavy barrage of mortar fire. In the next three days units of the Division and cavalrymen of the 11th Armored Cavalry Regiment killed 174 North Vietnamese Army regulars.

During this period, on 13 September, the Division Commander, General Ware, was killed in action. His command helicopter was shot down by hostile fire while he was directing operations against an estimated 1500 NVA troops near Loc Ninh. The Command Sergeant Major, Joseph A. Venable, and six others also died in the crash.

On 13 September Major General Orwin C. Talbott moved up from his position of Assistant Division Commander to assume command of the Division.

By the end of 1968, five BIG RED ONE soldiers received the Medal of Honor in the Vietnam War. The operations conducted by the Division have but one mission: seek out the enemy and destroy his ability and will to wage war.[4]

August 13, 1967

Dear Mom and Dad,

How's everything going? Thanks for sending those addresses of the guys. So, it's getting hot? I'm glad you had a good day for Coney Island. About that camera, I will buy a Polaroid this pay day and will begin sending pictures home.

You don't have to worry about the fighting down here in the south. The real heavy fighting is going on around the north (by the Marines) and that's 70 miles from here. That was pretty cute about Judy's handwriting (next time tell Jerri to hold her hand a little tighter).

You are right about water being deep over here. I went through a rice paddy and the water went up to my chest. The one bad thing is that the water is stagnant, and the mosquitos lay like a blanket covering the water. It usually takes 4 to 6 days for letters to get here. It all depends how the mail clerk feels that day, if the mail gets to you soon or late.

About the food over here. Most of it's good. It's not like home cooking but it keeps you alive. We have 3 hot meals a day unless I go

out on the line. Rice and potatoes are a must every meal. We have lousy meat and usually skip this. We have desserts (mostly when the Red Cross girls come around).

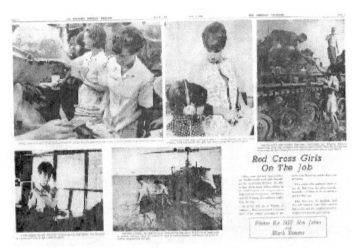

I've stayed about the same on my weight oh, somewhere between 165-175. The problem is drinks. We have tea which is pretty good (but who likes warm tea, when it's supposed to be cold). The milk usually sours within a mealtime. They do sell cold beer and Coke. This is the relief for the heat. What kills me is that now their "winter" months and they say around February they have the heat. But now the rain cools things off, and then it won't cool off, it'll stay hot. You don't have to send anything for my birthday because I don't need anything. If you send food, it will spoil, and if you send something that's of value, someone will steal it.

I've got a few things to send home, but the post office is so far away, it will be a while before I send them. Well, I better be going, it's time to eat and I want to get this letter off today and the guy is coming around to collect it. So, tell everybody I said hello. Take care and don't worry.

Jack

P.S. Tell Jerri Happy Birthday and tell Dad and the kids I said hello. Tell Jeff to add this coin to his collection. I hate to trouble you, but Bill's and Bob's addresses got wet and faded. Would you please send them again and Paul's if you can find it? Thanks.

ENLISTED MAN'S CLUB

Danger Forward, Volume 3, Issue 2, Pub. Date September 1, 1969,
Collection:1st Infantry Division Publications—Vietnam
RRMRC Digital Collection

August 1967

Dear Mom and Dad,

Things are going pretty slow now. Not much going on.

We bought a TV set. It's peculiar, but all they have is one station. And all they show are American shows. Perry Mason, Smothers' Brothers Show, Baseball, and many others.

I'm sending a few more propaganda sheets the helicopters drop out of their hatches. Also, a Vietnamese coin. I'm going down to Saigon Saturday for a day pass. We've been having classes on physical hygiene. Discussing the snakes, body diseases (such as jungle rot, trench foot, malaria, dysentery, food poisoning, leeches, venereal disease and ringworms). It was a very constructive and informative class.

One thing did happen though. Approximately last Monday morning at 2:30 am to 4:30 am, we had a mortar alert sounded by a constant siren. We stayed 2 hours in bunkers with mud up to above our knees. It was raining torridly and was very miserable and to top it off, we weren't mortared. I should be thankful though, but they pick the most ungodly times to have these alerts. You are either eating or at a show or at an EM club. One good thing over here is the EM (Enlisted Men) club. They bring bands from Saigon, Korea, Philippines, and even one from Hawaii.

I probably will buy a tape recorder and will be sending tapes home accompanied with letters. You can hear them on John's tape recorder and if you have time maybe buy a tape and record on it and maybe send it over here. Tapes are about 60 cents over here and it doesn't cost anything to send them to the states. It's better than letters and it lasts longer. Man, it is raining now. But at least it cools things down. So, you're having hot weather. It's not too hot now because it's winter over here (if you want to call it that). Their snow is daily

rain and it gets as cold as 75 degrees. Usually it's around 85-90 degrees during the day. But like I said before, it's winter over here. During the dry months (which is their summer) it gets as high as 120-130 degrees. Thanks for getting Bill's and Bob's addresses. Thank Jerri for the cards and letters. They were very interesting and amusing.

If you need any money, take it out of the bank. Because what I put in the Soldiers deposit over here will be entirely enough to get a car when I get out. And the Army will pay for all the education and my bonds will give me enough. So, I'll be sending another $150 at the end of this month, and I put $100 in the Soldiers deposit to get 10% interest. And when I'm a Specialist-4 (which will be in about 2-3 months) I'll put $200 in. About the bonds, I'm increasing them too. But I have to see at the end of the month to arrange that double name on the bond. I don't think it will be too much trouble. Combat pay goes up to $95 next month. Well I must be going. It's chow time. The food is pretty good. We won't be eating out of C-ration cans for quite a while yet. Tell everybody I said hello.

Love,

Jack

1ˢᵀ INFANTRY DIVISION CIVIC ACTION IN VIETNAM

Civic action in Vietnam was a major concern of the 1ˢᵗ Infantry Division. Behind a shield of American and Vietnamese combat operations, an up-to-date pacification program was conducted.

The primary goal of the nation building project, also known as Revolutionary Development — was to work with the government of South Vietnam in gaining the people's support for their Army and their government. Units of the BIG RED ONE were active in more than 30 projects encompassing every facet of civil affairs, all of which were designed to strengthen the nation. There were three phases of Revolutionary Development in which the 1ˢᵗ Infantry Division participated: Phase I, securing an area from the enemy Phase II, improving the secure environment economically and socially and Phase III, strengthening and unifying the grass-roots government for more effective operation in support of the Republic of Vietnam's central government. Along with combat strength, psychological operations helped build security by weakening the enemy's will to resist. PSYOPS, as the term was abbreviated, included dispersing leaflets, broadcasting from helicopters and educating civilians—all had the purpose of encouraging Viet Cong to rally or Chieu Hoi. Many ralliers were already active in the Division's Kit Carson program which trained the men to become scouts.

One man gave the following account of his transition: "My family lived under communist control for more than ten years, and I was forced to work for the Viet Cong. I was constantly afraid of being hit by American artillery, and I was seldom allowed to see my wife, even though I was a local guerrilla.

"Then I found a Chieu Hoi pass dropped by an American helicopter. My wife and some friends told me that it would be good to be a Hoi Chanh (a person who has rallied), but I hesitated for many weeks. "One day I came back from an operation to find that my wife had taken our children to Lam Son, out of Viet Cong reach. So, with the pass sewed to the lining of my shirt, I waited for my chance to escape North Vietnamese Army control and turned myself over to the American GIs. "Since then I have been trained to do scout work. I can see my wife and children every week and am happy working with the 1st Division soldiers."

Once an area was secured, health and living conditions of the civilians improved. Most civic action programs in the Division were associated with the second phase of Revolutionary Development through projects demanding immediate attention and by fostering long-range self-help programs. The most outstanding examples of immediate improvement were the Medical Civic Action Programs (MEDCAPS). Those projects were designed to show an interest in the people through medical aid and assistance.

MEDCAPS often became a featured part of hamlet festivals, which were intended to aid the Vietnamese people as well as give them a holiday. In addition to the medical treatment, food was served, and entertainment was provided by the 1st Division Band and American and Vietnamese cultural drama teams. Folk songs were sung about the soldiers in Vietnam, and efforts were made to recruit Hoi Chanhs (enemy VC soldiers who surrendered to the American forces).

Civil affairs coordination with agencies of the South Vietnamese government was essential at every level from the central government to individual villages. Everything in a program aimed to help and please citizens for the "nation building" objective to be realized. The plan's success was evidenced by the freedom of travel along Highway 13, less enemy harassment in villages, families who again had a place to live, and mostly in the beaming faces of children educated under a system which fostered the growth of democracy.[5]

CHAPTER THREE

MID-SUMMER 1967

GETTING HIS FEET WET

By mid-August 1967, Jack had been in Vietnam about a month. He continued learning about his situation and indicated heat, rain and mud are constant companions which contributed to fungal infestations so Jack's focus on good personal hygiene was something he wrote about several times.

Jack's best Army friend was killed during a mortar attack. Friendship was important to Jack and I was told he had a couple of good buddies in high school. They stayed in touch while he was in Vietnam and one continues sending holiday greetings to my mother. Jack also started to acknowledge the value of minding teachers and an academic education since the war might continue past the time our youngest brother could be drafted.

He wanted to be a helicopter gunner since he discovered he liked flying and it could bring a promotion and higher pay, but that will change. He sees Viet Cong prisoners and a base camp for the first time. Red Cross girls occasionally visited and cooked for his unit, but he was concerned about Detroit riots. Jack also focused on comradery and weapon maintenance which he knew affected morale and fighting success.

The Vietnamese poverty and fear made Jack sad although he met a beautiful native girl and I like to think they dated and had good times together. He was devastated when he saw a child cut open and commented about the mounting mental strains caused by war.

Jack volunteered for ambush patrols so he could earn his Combat Infantry badge and discovered he liked doing them since he learned more about field conditions. Jack felt the most dangerous times for a soldier were the first 3 and last 2 months in the country.

Jack started experiencing more action and continued getting very familiar with his environment which helped him survive as the war progressed.

Soldiers crossing streams between paddies

August 1967

Dear Mom and Dad,

Things are going fine now. All we have are classes and details. I'm burnt to a crisp. We went out and went to a few bars and had a few drinks. You ought to smoke a Vietnamese cigarette. There's so much dope in them that they're too strong to smoke. What really makes them taste so bad is that their tobacco is grown in cow manure.

It's still raining.

The only news I have that is worth much is that the other company we came over with on the boat was hit. It was a massacre. The base camp where they went was hit by mortar. They made their mistake in hiding under trucks instead of their bunkers and were blown up. 85% casualties were reported and 23 were killed. The hardest thing about it was that the best friend I had in the Army was killed. He was a real good guy and I don't think he could have killed a fly. It's a real shame. Just six days in Vietnam and the parents get a letter in the mail telling them that their son was killed. The thing about it is that our company was originally the ones that were supposed to be sent there. But for some strange reason the Captains changed their minds and sent them there and us here.

I saw a little child cut open by the terrorists. It was sad. That's the terrible thing about this war. The people are controlled by fear. They don't know what to think or do. The Viet Cong come in and kill and destroy and threaten. Then the Americans come in and bomb and kill. The people are so confused they don't know what to do. These people are really quiet and beautiful, but they are just as deadly if you underestimate them.

It's so sad to see the condition of the people. The women fight over pieces of plastic bags the supply room tosses away.

The men and women bicker over scraps off our plates. They are barefoot and wear clothes like American pajamas. They smell like animals and act like little dogs. They come up to my stomach and are very polite. They bow and thank you for everything. The women try to sell themselves for 2 or 3 dollars, but I can't see that. The situation over here is really drastic. Instead of spending a billion dollars a year fighting, we should spend the money helping the people.

Those riots in Detroit are terrible, 35 killed. If people want to fight, they should come over here. How's Jeff's eye? How's Jim and Jeff's baseball coming along? Did Jerri get her scholarship? Don't be backward about taking the money out of the bank if she doesn't get it.

I've got a long while before I get out of the service and I'm putting $125 a month in that Soldier's Deposit, and I'll raise that to $225 dollars when I get to be Specialist in about 4 months. The money draws 10% interest. I also raised my bond to $18.25 taken out a month.

Did you get that money and letters? How's the dog problem coming along? Tell Dad I said hello. And tell him I saw some real dandy stuff for you and him which I'm going to send home Christmas. We bought a cooler for 10 bucks and we keep the beer and Cokes cold by buying ice by the month for 2 dollars. I'm sorry I can't write very well but I'm writing by candlelight. The ants are terrible. They eat you out of house and home.

We have some Red Cross girls come out now and then to cook us food but not too often. Well my eyes are hurting so don't worry I'm fine and, in a way, enjoying myself. And remember if Jerri needs that money, use it.

Tell everyone I said hello.

Love, Jack

PSYOPS CIVIC ACTION

AN APPEAL is made by a PSYOPS team in a drive to recruit Hoi Chanhs, many of which rally and become active in the Division's Kit Carson program.

AN APPEAL meets with success.

SP-927 AIR-DROPPED PROPAGANDA LEAFLETS

Jack sent home this leaflet was produced by US (Psychological Warfare Operations) and is one of many varieties produced during the Vietnam war to reduce the morale of the North Vietnamese soldiers and civilian population.

TRANSLATION:

FRONT: Return to your family! They miss you and need you.

BACK: COMRADES OF THE VIET-CONG - COME HOME!

Your family needs you. They fear for your health and welfare. They know you will die if you do not heed their plea. The Government also wants you to come home. Contact the nearest Government of Vietnam soldiers and officials. You will be well treated, and both you and your family will be helped as soon as you return to the Just Cause.

DON'T DELAY. COME HOME!!

DETROIT UPRISING OF 1967: JULY 23-28

The Uprising of 1967 is also known as the Detroit Rebellion of 1967 and the 12th Street Riot. It began following a police raid on an unlicensed bar, known locally as a "blind pig." Over the course of five days, the Detroit police and fire departments, the Michigan State Police, the Michigan National Guard, and the US Army were involved in quelling what became the largest

civil disturbance in twentieth century America. The crisis resulted in forty-three deaths, hundreds of injuries, almost seventeen hundred fires, and over seven thousand arrests.

The insurrection was the culmination of decades of institutional racism and entrenched segregation. For much of the twentieth century, the city of Detroit was a booming manufacturing center, attracting workers—both black and white—from southern states. This diversity aggravated civil strife, and the

Riot of 1943 highlighted the racial fault lines that crisscrossed the city. Throughout the 1950s, homeowners' associations, aided by Mayors Albert Cobo and Louis Miriani, battled against integrating neighborhoods and school.

Deindustrialization within the city limits took many jobs to outlying communities, even as several auto companies went out of business. The east side of Detroit alone lost over 70,000 jobs in the decade following World War II. Construction of the city's freeways, newer housing, and the prospect of further integration—due to the demolition of the city's two main black neighborhoods, Black Bottom Valley—caused many whites to depart for the suburbs. From 1950 to 1960, Detroit lost almost 20 percent of its population.

Virginia Park transformed from a predominantly Jewish neighborhood to primarily black neighborhood by 1967. The new epicenter of black retail in Detroit became 12th Street (now called Rosa Parks Boulevard), a strip which also supported a lively illicit nightlife. Adding to tensions was the black community's fractious relationship with the mostly white Police Department. Like many forces across the country, the department was known for heavy-handed tactics and antagonistic arrest practices, particularly toward black citizens.

At 3:15am on July 23rd, the vice squad of the Detroit Police Department executed a raid on a blind pig at 12th Street and Clairmount. Despite the late hour, the avenue was full of people attempting to stay cool amidst a stifling heat wave. As the police escorted party goers to the precinct for booking, a crowd gathered, and the situation grew increasingly antagonistic. When the final arrestees were loaded into police vans, a brick shattered the rear window of a police cruiser, prompting a rash of break-ins, burglaries, and eventually arson.

Law enforcement was immediately overwhelmed. While the department had 4,700 officers, only about 200 were on duty at that hour. Early efforts to regain control failed and a quarantine of the neighborhood was imposed. Hoping to ease tensions, Mayor Jerome Cavanagh ordered that looters not be shot; as the word of his order spread, so did looting. The Michigan State Police and the National Guard arrived to reinforce police and fire units. Clashes between the mayor and Governor

George Romney—both of whom had presidential aspirations—and President Lyndon Johnson increased confusion and delayed the deployment of federal troops.

By the end of the first two days, fires and looting were reported across the city. Additionally, the mass theft of firearms and other weaponry turned Detroit into an urban warzone. Sniper fire sowed fear and hindered firefighting and policing efforts. The arrival of battle-tested federal troops on Tuesday, July 25th brought order.

For many people the uprising was a turning point for the city. White flight in 1967 doubled to over 40,000 and doubled again the next year. Yet, many Detroiters remained. The city saw a massive growth in activism and community engagement. New Detroit and Focus: HOPE were both founded in the aftermath, with the goal of addressing root causes of the disorder. As the city's demographics continued to shift, Detroiters elected the first black mayor in the city's history, Coleman A. Young.[6]

JACK CONSIDERED BECOMING A HELICOPTER GUNNER

August 1967

Dear Mom and Dad,

I'm sending you those booklets on Guam. I promised to send in the first letter. It finally stopped raining but now it is so humid it's hard to breathe. Did you get the other letters yet? I'm buying a Polaroid camera, so you'll be getting some pictures of Vietnam in about a week.

All the base camps in the 1ˢᵗ Division were hit last night except for ours, maybe someone is praying or living right. We have the safest base camp in Vietnam. There is so much heavy artillery, mortars, copters and planes that Charlie won't dare mortar or attack us.

We have some clod from the sticks in our unit. His whole body is covered with jungle rot. This is a fungus which grows on any scratch or callous (especially on your feet and arms). Mostly it's from not taking a bath or taking care of yourself. You must take care of yourself or the disease over here will kill you. Some of these kids don't shower even when they have a shower right here.

It's just like the states on the radio, only that they play a lot of old songs (mostly because they can't get a hold of any new ones) and a lot of hillbilly music. We have a counterpart of Hanoi Hanna. She's some girl from California who's on the radio and tries to make you feel at home. You should hear old Hanoi Hanna. She sounds like a man and just talks about how we should leave and how many men were killed or wounded, something like Tokyo Rose during the Second World War.

I like riding in helicopters immensely. There's something about them that takes your breath away. I really would like to be a gunner on them. I could make Sergeant fast plus I could get combat pay (which I'm making now) plus hazardous duty pay and flight pay. I put my 1049 for it. They've got me working in an office collect-

ing material for a book we're going to put out on the 1st Division around December. I'll send it home when it gets printed. It should be pretty nice.

Well let me collect myself. It is now raining.

The thing you really must watch out for over here is crotch itch, which is simply your underclothing rubbing against your body and getting irritated to where ringworm sets in and climbs down your leg. It's very annoying and painful. Another thing you have to watch out for is bamboo poisoning which is when you scratch yourself on bamboo and some of the poison enters the scratch and makes the limb swell twice its normal size. If you let it go, they must amputate the affected limb. Lastly is jungle rot. Which is like I said previously that is a fungus that grows on any part of your body. They said everybody will get it at some time or another (but some get it worse than others) because it thrives in a moist, humid area and you get so wet and stay wet, that you can't help but get it.

How's everybody doing? Did Jerri get her scholarship? How's Jim and Jeffs baseball coming around? Tell them to keep practicing. How's the house? The neighbors?

When are they going to stop those riots? That Detroit ought to be thrown out. Cincinnati is starting up again in Hamilton, isn't it? I have a boy in my platoon who is from Silverton. His brother teaches at U.C. His name is Bill and he teaches at A&S. This guy went to U.C. in Music Conservatory. He can really play the piano. He went a year and enlisted.

Well I better go. So, don't worry, I'm fine. Tell everyone I said hello.

Love,

Jack

P.S. I'm also sending you a card commemorating the day and time we crossed the International Date Line.

GUAM PAMPHLETS SENT HOME BY JACK

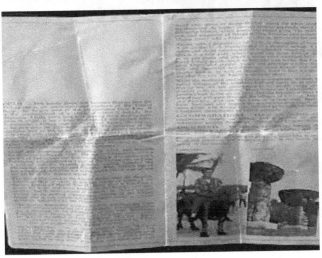

AMBUSH PATROLS

August 1967

Dear Mom and Dad,

Well it's been a few days since I wrote so I figure I'd drop a few lines.

I went out on an ambush the other night. The only thing is we didn't see any VC but almost got mortared by our own men. Two mortars hit around 20 meters from our position and man what a scare we had. The mortars were whizzing over our heads and suddenly, the whizzing was louder and kept getting louder then suddenly a crash and I never was so scared in my life. There was nowhere to go, and you hug the ground like it's covered with money. Then the others came and it's closer. You think the only thing left then is to say your prayers.

But the Lieutenant called up top and told them they were a little off target.

For days now all it's done has been raining. I thought the camp would have floated away. It's still raining. I got three letters from Bob G. Two cards and a long letter. They sent me 15 bucks and I would appreciate if you would call them up and maybe have them come over to see the house. If you don't want them to that's all right. Bob's still in the seminary and will start his second year in college.

How's things going? Did Jerri get her scholarship? If she needs any money tell her to use the money in the bank. Well I best be going because I don't have much more to say. All I have to say is that I'm fine and have everything I need so don't worry. Tell everybody I said hello.

Love,

Jack

COMMANDERS CALLING
ARTILLERY STRIKES

August 22, 1967

Dear Mom and Dad,

How are things going? Oh, it's going fairly well here. I saw a helicopter get shot down. It was about 200 meters away and a mortar hit it and it fell like a rock. It was pretty gruesome to see the crew members after it hit. After we got the fire out, we had to take the bodies out. It was pretty sad. The only other dead person I've seen was a little child that was cut open and headless.

But to change to more pleasant thoughts, a Captain friend of mine went home yesterday. Boy did he throw a party. A good thing I found out was that you can put a 5-cent stamp on the letter to here and it will go air mail. Just don't put it in an air-mail envelope or put air mail on the outside.

The only major problem I have really is getting clean laundry. We have a Vietnamese laundry and it's only 20-cents for a set of fatigues, but the only thing is that they don't come clean and they smell so. They smell worse after you get them back than before you sent them.

The funniest thing that's happened so far is that a little old man who's a disc jockey at the station is marrying some young Vietnamese girl with 6 kids. I don't know. Another interesting fact is the age factor over here. The young ones (around 9-13) you'll think they're 8 or younger. The young kids are cute. The young ones look so sickly. All of them are thin and puny. There is no middle age (it seems). Between 22-40, the people either look younger or older than their actual age. It depends mainly on your social level how fast your age progresses. I'll tell you one thing; this climate over here has great effects. You just sweat like a hog, even if you walk only to the mess hall. If you don't drink a lot of water, you're running a good chance to be a heat casualty.

Tomorrow I'm going out on an ambush. I volunteered for it. I just want to get a chance and earn my CIB (Combat Individual Badge). This is a rifle with a wreath around it with a blue field behind it. The only way to earn it is to be under actual fire and I want to have the experience (maybe I'll even get the chance to get a Charlie).

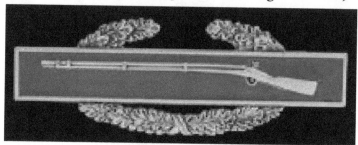

Well how are things going? Did you like LeSourdsville? How's the kids going to like school? Did Jerri get her scholarship? I hope so. If she doesn't, be sure to use that money in the bank. I'll be sending some more home at the end of this month. Well I better get cleaning my .45 pistol and M-16 rifle, so don't worry.

Love,

Jack

P.S. Tell Dad and the kids and everyone I said hello. I'm sending the hat crest for this brigade. Also, I have a black beret I'm allowed to wear.

AUTOMATIC CLOTHES WASHER IN VIETNAM

VIET CONG ENEMY CAPTURE

DESTROYING HIS WILL TO FIGHT

This VC has had enough

During Operation ATTLEBORO, a surprise raid by the 3d Brigade *Rangers* on Ben Cat, proved successful

A *Ranger* keeps close watch on the detainees

Getting them out of their holes

August 1967

Dear Mom and Dad,

Not much doing around here but I did see my first Viet Cong. They were captured just outside the perimeter of the base camp. They were filthy and almost naked when captured but 3 days later they were cleaned up and well-clothed when I saw them next. They are sneaky and wonder who they are. One of them made a gesture to me with his hand, as to slit my throat, then laughed.

Prisoners are real problems over here. We can't just kill them (although that's what I think I would do). According to the book, you're supposed to take them prisoner, interrogate them and then turn them over to the South Vietnamese and try to rehabilitate them. The only thing is that the South Vietnamese take them in, feed them, give them medical attention, clothe them, and then put them in the Army. The only thing is that they turn around, take off well-clothed and fed and even take the weapon and just go back to the VC. To make things worse, they use the tactics of the South Vietnamese (which are primarily the same as ours) and use them against us.

I tell you one thing; I wouldn't blink an eye to shoot one of these VC and think nothing of it. If you don't, they just go back, better educated, and healthy to the VC and he might just be the man who kills you.

The Americans are too soft on the VC. They laugh and make fun of our generosity. I hate them all.

Sorry about the slanted handwriting but I hardly have any light. Some nut across from me sent a letter to a lonely-hearts club and is reading a list of names and how much each woman's bank account is worth. He's been married two times and is only 19. It's raining really hard now. The worst since I've been here. If you walk out the tent, you'll sink knee deep in mud.

Tell Jim not to act up in school and tell him that it's fun and to behave. Tell Jeff to stay like he is (like Jerri) and he'll be alright. Tell Judy not to eat and drink so much at LeSourdsville Lake or she'll get herself sick again. Did Jerri get her scholarship yet? If she didn't, tell her to use the money in the bank. Tell Dad not to be such a speed demon (HA HA) and to wait before crossing those orange lights (HA HA). Only kidding. Dad's the safest driver on the road and the cops should spend taxpayer's money stopping real speeders and some of those people rioting instead of giving a stupid ticket to a law-abiding citizen.

I'm doing fine over here and like I said before I like it over here so don't worry. I don't need a thing and am well fed (HA HA) and well taken care of. I must be going. It's time for lights out. So have fun at LeSourdsville and tell the kids to be good and don't worry. Tell everyone I said hello.

Love,

Jack

Jack and comrade in the jungle

MONSOON SEASON

August 1967

Dear Mom and Dad,

Well I got paid this past Wednesday, but the only thing is that they screwed up the records and they owe me $162. I'm going down this afternoon and get things straightened out, and about me sending too much home, you don't have to worry about me sending too much home because I really don't need that much. I really can't spend it on too many things and if I send it home it will mean more money in the bank and the better things to have when I get back to the states. I don't go out that much and I wouldn't spend it on foolish things and if I keep it, somebody will probably steal it.

I have no problem with my money. I told them to put $100 a month in the Soldiers Deposit Savings where it will draw 10% interest so when I get this month's money (the allotment doesn't start until September) I'll send a $150 home. Could you please tell me how much I have in the bank?

Well promotion time is almost here; in a few weeks I'll be a Specialist 4 Class and be making $250 a month. Then I'll raise my allotment to $200 a month and I'm hoping before I leave this place to be a Sergeant but that's far, far off yet. All I need a month is about 40 or 50 dollars and don't tell me I need any more.

I saw a nifty jacket for Jim and Jeff. It has sewn in the back the phrase "I should go straight to heaven when I die, cause I've done spent my time in hell." Also included is a large picture of Vietnam.

Flash! The big rumor is that we might get sent up to War Zone C next week. That's pretty thick up there with Charlie. But it's just rumors. Rumors are so thick. Another rumor is that we're going to Pleiku to protect the people so they can vote. Those elections are coming up. There's going to be plenty of bombs and mortars flying for this election. The ones you must watch ae the ARVINS (the South Vietnamese soldiers), half of these are VC and have orders to blow up things and cause confusion among the people. I might get to go to Saigon and interview a few people, but I hope not.

I really enjoy the ambushes and patrols they let me go out on. It gets pretty wet on these ambushes and they think I'm crazy to ask to go on them, but you know how bad it is when you go out on these different missions. I'm glad to be attached to the Infantry. I have the greatest respect for the Infantrymen.

You should see these kids over here. A six-year-old kid smokes cigarettes like a twenty-year-old. They really love that chewing gum. I'm sorry I haven't written more but I was at Cameron Bay making some reports and didn't have any time. You might think that sounds funny, but I was swamped day and night. For the five days I was there I had a total of 20 hours sleep.

About those patrols. I went through my first VC base camp the day before yesterday. You'd have to see it to believe it. Their tunnel systems are ingenious. It's hard to believe that these lazy people can build enormous tunnel complexes. We didn't encounter any VC resistance (thank God) but we did find 3 old women without ID's and took them in (we did find out later that they were VC). The only thing if you capture a VC (which is more trouble than it's worth, the best thing is to shoot them) they're put in a brainwashing school with the ARNINS (South Vietnamese) for 6 weeks and then set free again. You just can't win. Well you have to excuse the handwriting, but it is done by candlelight. I better get running along. It is 12 o'clock and I got to get some sleep. Don't worry and tell everyone I said hello.

Love,

Jack

P.S. You should get a tape in the mail soon.

VIET CONG BASE CAMP/TUNNEL COMPLEX

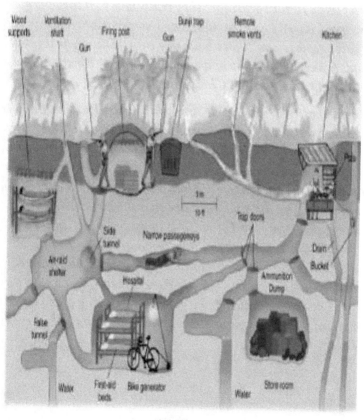

August 1967

Dear Mom and Dad,

You have to excuse my handwriting because I'm writing to you by candlelight. I am still doing fine. I really like this place the longer I stay, but I'm dissatisfied with my job. I dislike sitting on my can while others are doing all the fighting. I've made friends with two Bronze Star winners. One is a Vietnamese policeman and the other is a medic. The Vietnamese policeman (Vaking) is now an ARVIN (an ally of Americans) and is a translator and won his Bronze Star by exposing himself to direct fire and killing three Viet Cong.

The medic Charlie T. won his Bronze Star by saving a man who was shot in the throat and performed a tracheotomy on the field under fire. I really would like to put in for a machine gunner on a helicopter. The only thing is that I'll have to spend another six months over here. But I don't think I'll mind that too much, and I get $2000 as a bonus if I sign up for another six months plus getting combat pay, Sergeant's pay, and aviation pay. As of now I will go out in the field with my .45 pistol and M-16 and see much action. A friend of mine caught a bullet in the chest and he's going home. Another one is getting sent home for mental reasons. He froze up when they were on patrol and went crazy and tried to shoot himself.

There is a definite mental strain over here because there isn't any place that is really safe. Oh, they might have guards and barbed wire fence up, but it really isn't safe. Charlie lets himself known occasionally, when he puts a mine here and there, or puts a Claymore (a mine) set up in a Vietnamese bar or store. We had an incident last week where they put a Claymore in a Vietnamese gook store. It killed only one American and he was going home in 3 weeks. The most dangerous time over here is your first 3 months and your last 2. Because when you first get here, Charlie wants to test you and if you don't beat him, he will walk all over you. And in your last months, you might become too overconfident and think that since you've lasted this long, Charlie won't touch you. This is where they make their mistake.

This is a good place to be. All other base camps of the First Division have been hit except for here at Di An. Some of the boys I came over with are already dead. Even my best friend.

I won't have to be worried about mortars too much (except for alerts), although 2 mortars hit at the north east section of the base last week. We have a boy with jungle rot (which incidentally Rocky has). On your feet it is exceptionally painful. I just hope Rocky doesn't have trench foot. If he does and has it bad enough, sections of his feet will rot away such as toes, skin, toenails etc. This will affect him for life, so I hope it isn't this.

The ants over here are carnivorous. They love human flesh. They build tremendous ant hills which are shaped like a miniature volcano. You can hear the buzzing-like sound of the thousands of ants. In minutes they crawl over their prey and literally eat it.

The Viet Cong use this as a little tactic of torture. They stick your whole body in one of these 'holes' and "persuade" you to divulge information. The only thing is if you talk, they won't take you out and if you don't talk, they still leave you in there.

I saw a dead man today. He was a Viet Cong and was killed by the 16th Infantry. It's sad to see this. It shouldn't be but that's the way war is. I'm just glad that America isn't like this place. The people are so corrupted, they'd sell their daughters or sisters to you for 500 pens. ($5.00). I met a very nice Vietnamese girl (from a well-educated and wealthy Vietnamese family). She is well-spoken in English and is watched over by momashon and papashon (mama and papa). She has some French in her and is beautiful in Vietnamese standards. Her name is Mia V. She is the most decent Vietnamese I've met. If all the Vietnamese were like her, we wouldn't have to be over here now. I am a sort of outsider around here. I don't go out every night and waste my money on trivial things. When these wasted things (common women) come up to me, I tell them to beat it instead of flashing my money around and buying "expensive" *things, expensive in Vietnam, but junk in America. I seem not to fit in the hard ways of war, but in a way, I like it. I like it because it's different. You'll never imagine how it feels. It's beyond description.*

You can help people so easily if you just stop and take the time. It is a wonderful feeling to have people thank you humbly for things so simple, that people in America would laugh at the way they accept it. All it takes is maybe a minute of your time. I received all your letters and Jerri's. I really enjoyed them. About that Bond, I have to wait until the end of the month on payday. You'll get another check at the end of the month for about the same amount. Combat pay is rising in October from $65 to $95, so that's more money.

How's Jerri and the lifeguard doing? Tell him I said hello. If Jerri doesn't get her scholarship use the money in the bank. I got a card from John and Grandma. Tell them thanks. Jerri should be getting a present at the end of the month, if I can get it mailed. Well tell everyone I said hello. I must be going because my pen is running out of ink. It is now raining so hard that the tent is ready to fall down. I'm sending a propaganda slip we drop in villages. So, don't worry. Take care.

Love.

Jack

P.S. Picture's not very good. How do you like the beret? HA HA

PSYOPS LEAFLET DROP

SP-941A DROPPED PROPAGANDA LEAFLETS

Jack sent home this leaflet that was produced by US (Psychological Warfare Operations) and is one of many produced during the Vietnam War to reduce the morale of the N. Vietnamese soldiers and civilian population.

TRANSLATION:

TO THE SOLDIER IN THE RANKS OF THE VIET CONG

We miss you. Do you remember us? Do you ever think of your family? You know the GVN forces are winning everywhere. I worry about you. Where are you? What has happened to you? The Open Arms policy of the GVN will welcome your return to us. I hope this letter reaches you in time and that you will make up your mind to return to us. TET is approaching. Return and enjoy a happy TET with us. I am waiting for you, hoping for your safe return.

BIG RED ONE CIVIC ACTION

*Vietnamese youngsters get a ready hand in helping build a school
in which they will soon be studying.*

FIELD LIFE

August 24, 1967

Dear Mom and Dad,

I received your letter about Jerri getting her scholarship and I'm very happy. If she needs any money for clothes or for the car use the money in the bank. It came in the nick of time.

Nothing much happening here except I saw the most ironic thing yesterday. A boy was drinking in the EM (Enlisted Men's) club and I guess he drank too much, and it affected his heart, he collapsed and plainly suffocated to death. He turned pale then blue and gasped a few times for air then a guy jumped on him and gave him mouth-to-mouth resuscitation, but it did no good. He died a minute and a half after he collapsed. The funny thing, two medics were there but they were so drunk, they couldn't help him and here's where the irony comes in, the band there was playing- guess what – "Oh When the Saints Come Marching In." That was the first man I ever saw who literally drank himself to death. It is such a shame to have your parents or wife get a letter from the Army informing you that your son died of drinking himself to death, but they won't tell them that. They'll put it down as a non-combatant casualty. You'd think he would have known better.

Tell Jerri if she has an English class it would be quite a short story to write. I saw my first VC base camp. We found a bicycle and an animal trap. We also took a woman in who didn't have an ID. These base camps are really elaborate and contain punji pits (holes with sharp sticks sticking up – usually poisoned with animal waste). You really had to watch where you stepped, or you'd end up with one less foot. You'd have to see these unique underground bunkers and tunnels. It's hard to believe that these slow moving, lazy people could work on these tunnels and build these enormous complexes. I got a bullet-proof vest the other day for when I go into town or out in the field. They gave me plenty of ammo for my .45 pistol and I'm all set.

I have an appointment tomorrow with finance to work out that deal of the bond. There should be no problem. Also, this payday you'll probably get another check. I get back combat pay (do you know I've almost been out here three months. Time goes fairly fast here, that's why it isn't so bad.

By the way, how's Rocky doing? I hope well. If you need any money for the car, use the money in the bank. That's good you bought that dryer. It makes things a lot easier. Aren't those Reds something? I don't know what their problem is. Well I better be going. Tell everyone I said hello. Give my congratulations to Jerri on her scholarship. How are the kids set for school? Don't worry and I'll write again soon.

Love,

Jack

Viet Cong tunnel

A TOUCH OF HOME:
VISIT FROM MISS AMERICA

Page 8   THE AMERICAN TRAVELER   August 20, 1967

Miss America And Her Court Visit Div

Miss America and her court visited several from Brigade units. Shown (l to r) are: Miss Boise, Miss Ellen Warren; Miss South Carolina, Miss Barbara Harris; Miss America, Miss Jane Anne Jayroe; MG John H. Hay, Division Commander; Miss Alabama, Miss Angi Greene; Miss Wisconsin, Miss Sharon Braytock; COL Frederick Kranze, Chief of Staff and Miss Connecticut, Miss Ann Gelish.

'Miss America — Miss Jane Anne Jayroe from Oklahoma sings during a variety show at the Red Cross Center at the LoL Khe basecamp.

August 26, 1967

Dear Mom and Dad,

I got your letters and it's been a while since I received a letter. Mail service is screwed up. The planes aren't doing their jobs on delivering the mail. Maybe they'll straighten out. About those tapes. I first have to buy a recorder before I send any home.

I'm sorry to hear that Dad's got a cold. You're working too much. Take it easy, you're having hours like the service now. You'll probably be getting some more money (unless I buy a tape recorder) at the end of the month. I'm about to put my paper in to get that copter gunner and I wouldn't mind staying another 6 months or a year. You get 2000 dollars for every additional 6 months you extend plus all the pay you get. I could save close to 4-5 thousand bucks if I stay another year. I don't mind it here and since I have 18 months left after I leave Vietnam the first time it would be nice, because I hate to be in the Army in the states. We have a very nice chapel in our Brigade so that's no problem

Tell Jim to do his best in school and to obey the teacher. If he doesn't, he'll end up like his brother, because this thing might be going on when he gets my age. Bob G. said Skip S. (a boy who went to Purcell) had a 3-inch hole shot in his foot and is back in the states. And about those movies? We have movies every night and Vietnamese civilian bands almost every night. They try to make things as nice as possible. Miss America was down at the USO, but I didn't go down. And about the Forrestal carrier, I saw it prior to the sinking when we passed it about 50 miles out from Vietnam.

And take it easy Dad. You don't get that many vacations. Tell Mom to lay off those details. I found a new way of satisfying my thirst. We put Kool-Aid in a plastic 2-quart bag and drink it instead of water. That picture I sent was a joke. It's not as good as it seems to be. How'd you like the beret? Mine's black instead of green.

Well I've said too much anyway. I just thought it'd be good to drop a line. Tell Jim and Jeff good luck on their schoolwork. Tell Judy to be good. Tell Jerri to write again. I enjoyed her letters. Tell Dad I said hello and take it easy and thank him for his letter and ask him to write again. I heard from Dad you're considering a little trip to New York. If I were you, I'd go. That's one thing, you only have one life and the good Lord put the places there for man to see, so take advantage. See the world, join the Army. HA HA. That's what you ought to do, join the WAC. HA HA.

Love,

Jack

CHAPEL FOR SOLDIERS IN DI AN, VIETNAM

"...For A Vietnam Memorial"

Division members and guests leave the Memorial Chapel at Di An after its formal dedication August 14   Photo by Sp/4 Charles A. DePriest

CHAPTER FOUR

September 1967–More Action

After about 45 days in Vietnam Jack saw more action in the field. His unit encountered the enemy, exchanged fire, suffered casualties and killed several Viet Cong soldiers. He experienced many mortar attacks and continued going on ambush patrols since he felt he was 'doing something' although he froze at night.

This chapter has one letter Jack wrote to his fraternal twin. He was convinced she would get a college scholarship to help continue her studies although he repeated offers for her to use money in his bank account back home. He mentioned pricing cars and possibly buying one in Vietnam and having it shipped home. Cars were important to Jack and he left a large, red Chevrolet at home after he left for Vietnam. I remember talking to him, when he was home on leave, about his favorite models and he had his heart set on getting Dodge Roadrunner.

He repeated his intention to submit his request to be a helicopter machine gunner but in a subsequent letter decided not to since he saw a fiery helicopter crash and helped retrieve several dead bodies from the wreckage.

Jack had Army journalism training and was a line journalist for his unit. He wanted to study Political Science and wrote about extending his tour, indicating he would if he could get a job in the Army's Vietnam Civic action project which involved helping local people improve their lives. Jack cared about others and I learned he attended a Catholic seminary a few months while in High School. Apparently he considered priesthood but was challenged by the rigors encountered during that training especially committing to celibacy. Jack was also very interested in geopolitical affairs and he started mentioning potential 1968 US presidential candidates and their chances of winning the election.

R&R was a consistent theme during Jack's 1967 September, and he hoped to get time away in an exotic location. I include various R&R destinations with associated costs at the time for hotels, food, and transportation. He complained about leeches and I remember him talking to me when he was on leave, about how they felt on his skin and the discomfort they caused. Jack became friends with the unit's Vietnamese interpreter, and he continued focusing on weapon selection and maintenance since he knew there was more action in the months ahead.

September 1, 1967

Dear Mom and Dad,

Well I just thought I'd drop a line or two. That's really weird about that weather back in the states. That's too bad, August and September are the best months. Summer is too short for it to be ruined by cold weather. Watch when the kids get in the school, the weather will be so nice and it will get so hot, they won't be able to stand it.

That's great about Jeff and what the principal said. Tell Jim to behave and obey the teacher and do well. The school sounds pretty nice and modern.

I wouldn't send any money through the mail because it is censored and there will probably be a light-fingered son of a gun who would take it.

About those ambushes. Things do get crowded out in the boonies sometimes. There was a rumor about the First Division moving to another location farther north, but it will be around next May or June. About the ambushes, I plan to go out on another this Wednesday. The people think I'm crazy, but I feel like I'm doing something.

One good thing is that it won't be cold over here. It will be starting summer when it's the coldest over there. I really hate that Cincinnati weather. But it will be so hot you drink; they say about 8 quarts of water a day. I did write Bill a letter, but I guess it didn't get to him or he didn't answer it. I bought a large footlocker made of beer cans for $7.50 and that was the most expensive one. I have so much junk and clothes I still have to leave it in my duffel bag.

We had a mortar alert about 3:00 AM Tuesday night which lasted until 5:00 in the morning. There was water above your knees in some of them. I've made good friends with the interpreter for the company. His name is Giao and was put in for the Bronze Star for shooting a VC with his pistol. He was a Vietnamese policeman before he came to the Americans. He speaks English very well.

They made fun of me (which I don't mind) because I keep my weapons so clean. But I tell them the M-16 will jam if it's not kept clean (which is true). The weapon is very touchy when it becomes dirty. I don't trust it but if it's kept clean, it can chop a man in two. You see the bullet leaves the barrel, like any other, but when it reaches a certain distance, the projectile begins to tumble. It goes in easy enough and clean but the only thing it blows out most of your back when it leaves.

They also have a round that shoots two bullets with one shot and is used in the M-14 rifle. You can hit two birds with one stone.

Flash. We got the word in and it is confirmed. We will probably move within the next month to Da Nang around about 10 to 20 miles south of the DMZ, but I don't know.

Well I only got 3 more months before I put my 1049 in for machine gunner. That means more rank and money. Well I better get going. Tell the kids to be good. Tell Dad and Jerri I said hello. Take care and don't worry.

Love,

Jack

September 1967

Dear Jerri,

How's your second-year progressing? What are you taking this year? What new additions have you got over at U.C., or has it stayed the same?

I've got a few things to send home, but I've got to get paper and wrap them. They won't send them unless they're wrapped. Your letters are sent free, but they make that up by charging you so much to send packages. Something should be done about it.

That's great about those scholarships. If you need any money don't be hesitant in using any of my savings because I won't need it when I come back because if I get a job I really like over here, I'll extend until I get out of the Army. You get $1800 every time you extend for 6 months plus double combat pay. And if I make Specialist next month, I hope to leave here a Sergeant E-5 or better.

I was pricing cars the other day and they have a plan where you order your car over here and you get an eighteen per cent discount. What do you think would be the best model to get? They have all makes of cars. American cars are nice but I'm partial to those foreign sports cars. A Corvette is nice (and so is the price). I really like those Sprites or Lotus or Austin-Healey, but I have to take into consideration those costly repairs, but then "I tell myself; you only live once."

And I don't intend to get married and the Army will pay for my education. I would like to go to Villa Madonna and major in Political Science. The Army will pay for everything, even my room and board. If I don't extend, the Army has a plan to send you to the University of Maryland, but I don't know the details.

We are moving out to Quan Loi this Thursday and I don't know exactly what I'm going to do. I'll probably be up there for around two months. The only thing I'll have to watch out for is mortars. I'm pretty settled over here but now they're going to send up north 75 miles and I'll have to re-adjust myself.

The engineers are just beginning to build houses for us (we've been living in tents since I got here). It's hard to believe that I've been here 3 months going on the fourth. Time goes fairly fast over here. Around the 6th month I might go on R&R. There are numerous places you can go. There's Hawaii, Australia, New Zealand, Japan, Thailand, Singapore, Hong Kong, Taipei, Bangkok to mention just a few. I'd like to go to Japan or Taipei but if the expenses are too high, I'll just take a three-day pass to sleep. This is probably what I'll do.

How does Jim like school? Is Jeff doing good? I hope so. How's Judy doing? Is dad doing fine? Tell mom not to worry.

Well, I better be going. So, I hope you do real fine on your studies. Good luck.

Jack

CHRYSLER ADVERTISEMENT PUBLISHED IN "STARS AND STRIPES"

Town & Country 3-seat Station Wagon

Need a Car When You Get Home?

You can wash that back window without leaving the wheel. An optional wiper/washer inside the tail gate does it. Down.-Up. Cleaned!

These luxury wagons come two ways. In two- and three-seat versions. The "2" seater features a 10 cubic foot lockable storage compartment.

Getting the spare tire out—if you ever have to—is no problem. Lower the tail gate and remove the tire from its special compartment behind the right rear wheelwell. Town & Country tires are 8.85 x 14s to handle extra wagon weight with ease.

To see what other great ideas we have for you in the 1968 Stateside Delivery Program write to Box 1688, Detroit, Michigan 48231. If you think Chrysler means big money . . . you're in for a happy surprise.

EXPORT SALES DEPT.
P.O. BOX 1688
DETROIT, MICHIGAN

EXPORT-IMPORT DIVISION **CHRYSLER** CORPORATION

C RATIONS (COMBAT RATIONS)

C-Rations were developed in 1938 as a replacement for reserve rations, which sustained troops during World War I, and consisted chiefly of canned corned beef or bacon and cans of hardtack biscuits, as well as ground coffee, sugar, salt and tobacco with rolling paper—much in the way of variety. Researchers at

the Quartermaster Subsistence Research and Development Laboratory in Chicago went to work to design food products that could be kept for long time periods and were more delicious and nutritious than reserve rations. The design they came up with consisted of 12-ounce tinplate cans that were opened with a key. At first, the meals were stews, and more varieties were added as the war went on, including meat and spaghetti in tomato sauce, chopped ham, eggs and potatoes, meat and noodles, pork and beans, ham and lima beans, and chicken and vegetables.

Besides these main courses, chocolate or other candies, gum, biscuits and cigarettes were added.

When three meals a day were consumed, C-Rations provided about 3,700 calories. They could be eaten cold but tasted better cooked. Troop feedback on C-Rations often went unheeded. For instance, the ham and lima beans entree was unpopular, but it remained in the C-Ration mix until well into the Vietnam War. Two other complaints were that the food selection was monotonous, and the meals were heavy to carry into combat on foot. In 1958, C-Rations were replaced by "Meal, Combat, Individual" rations. The contents were almost identical to C-Rations, so they continued to be called C-Rats until the early 1980s, when "Meal, Ready-to-Eat" replaced them. MREs came in packages instead of cans, so they were much lighter than C-Rations.[7]

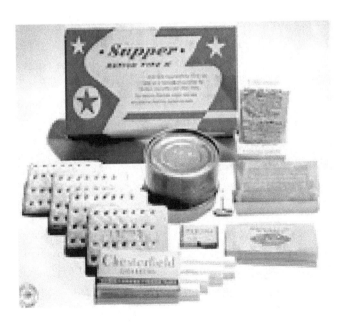

September 1967

Dear Mom and Dad,

Well things are pretty slow around here. I have one thing that's of importance. I'm moving up to Quan Loi this Thursday. I can't say exactly what I'm going to do but I couldn't if I did know. We should be up there for a month or two. Quan Loi is about 75 miles north of Saigon. It's near the Cambodian border.

Guys are going nuts over getting passes. I didn't take one and they think I'm crazy. They're all going into town and really "living it up" if you want to call it that. The next thing you know is they'll be running to the medics for shots to cure what they've picked up.

How are things back in the states? If Romney would run, I think he would win (at least over here) because Johnson would have at least 500,000 votes against him.

I'm sitting here eating C-rations. I "borrowed" them from the supply room. The main courses aren't too hot, let's see – a ham and lima beans, beef with spiced sauce but I also have a turkey meal (which incidentally is pretty good). The desserts are what I really like. There's pound cake in one, date pudding in another, pecan cake on another. I love those desserts.

How's Jim and Jeff doing in school? I hope well. That's too bad about Judy's teeth. I've got an appointment to get mine checked but with us moving out, I don't know if I'll be able to keep it.

How's Jerri like her second year at U.C.? I've been pricing different makes of cars. You see they have a plan where you get an 18% discount if you buy in Vietnam, a new car. It's only for servicemen. At the present I'm pretty partial to a new T-bird but I don't know. I was pricing some sport cars like Lotus, Sprite, or Corvette but those will run me pretty high. I'll probably end up buying a Volkswagen or a compact car.

I'm including a copy of the Vietnamese constitution. It might do good in school for somebody. How are things going? Good, I hope. The monsoon season is nearing its end and the dry season should be setting in around the end of November and early December. By then it will be so hot you can hardly stand it.

Well I better be going. Say hello to Dad and everybody. I'll probably write a few more letters before I leave for Quan Loi.

Love,

Jack

Car advertisement targeted at soldiers stationed in Vietnam

LEECHES

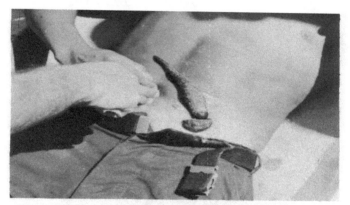

FIGURE 61.—Engorged buffalo leeches feeding on a volunteer. Salt has been poured on the leech in the foreground, causing it to shrivel and loosen its attachment to the skin.

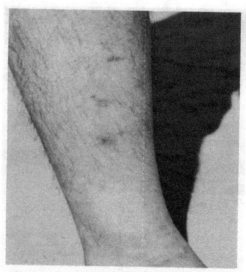

FIGURE 60.—Leech bite on the leg of an infantryman who had waded through a leech-infested paddy. Note the triradiate configuration caused by the three cutting plates in the leech's mouth.

September 1967

Dear Mom and Dad,

I'm sorry I haven't written you more recently, but I've been literally swamped with work. I am now up at Quan Loi around 60 miles north of Saigon, close to the Cambodian border and a few miles from the Black Virgin Mountains. Swamped in is really what I mean. You pick up leeches just walking to the mess hall. It rains so hard and long and the mud is so red, it's hard to stay clean. We do have the opportunity to take showers and change clothes regularly. If they didn't do this, guys would be coming down with all sorts of things.

I have had 5 leeches on me since I've been here and I'll tell you one thing, they're not too comfortable. The heat and humidity are treacherous in this part of the country. We had a guy collapse with a heart attack right on the road. He died. Malaria is beginning to strike a few guys in the different companies. We also had a jerk who almost shot his hand off with a .45 pistol.

You wouldn't believe the size of the ants, snakes, and spiders. When you go out on patrol, you walk near these ant hills and they almost drag you away and the spiders have webs stretched from trees to trees. I also saw a python snake that was 10 feet long.

Around here there is a little more VC influence. There is an estimated VC battalion roaming around out there but we just can't find them. We found a few VC mortar positions and many tunnels. They human-waved the place about three months ago but the only thing they accomplished was blowing up a truck with 4 fifty caliber machine guns mounted on it and killing nine men.

Going into the villages is something else. Ten out of every twelve houses are prostitute joints. The people overall are very friendly (mainly because they want your money). You can go into any house and eat, and they treat you very nice.

The thing is, is you can make money by selling soap, gum, cigarettes, spray deodorant, powder, you name it and they'll buy it. The thing is that they'll put it on the black market and sell it to the VC or someone for twice of what they gave you. There are women who stand everywhere you look, and they are selling Cokes. (I don't know where in the world they get Cokes, but they have them). They sell them for 30 cents a bottle. What a monopoly.

I got a new weapon to carry. I turned in my M-16 rifle for a modified M-14 AR (automatic rifle). It fires a magazine of 20 rounds in 10 seconds. The thing I like about it, is that it won't stop like that M-16 if it gets wet. I feel twice as safe as I did before. Plus, they have a new duplex round where two projectiles come from one bullet.

I felt bad when I didn't write because I don't want you to be worried, but I had a fever and wasn't up to par. I'm alright now.

How have you been? I've been receiving your letters regularly and it's been a morale booster. The kids are doing well in school, I hope. How does Jerri like her schedule? I'm sending another coin home for Jeff's collection. Well the rain is coming so I'm going. Take care.

Love,

Jack

September 26, 1967

Dear Mom and Dad,

Well I thought I'd just write a few lines since I haven't been too regular with my letters.

I'm still at Quan Loi but the rumor is that we will move either to Lai Khe, which is to the south by Di An or to War Zone C, near the Black Virgin Mountains, around 8 miles from here. If we move to the latter, I think we will see our first action with the Viet Cong. It doesn't matter much to me, but I hope it is Lai Khe. Lai Khe is fairly nice. A nice village and modern conveniences.

The rain and dust are really trying on your nerves. You're almost never clean and your boots stay wet almost all the time. A good thing about it is that we get these sundry packs containing cigarettes, candy, socks, and we get almost anything we need. Guys who haven't obtained the art of proper physical hygiene are coming down with jungle rot and VD. We usually eat two hot meals a day but when I'm out in the field, you get sea rations.

I just about put my order in for a Sunbeam (a Chrysler sports car). I would get it when I got home. The good thing is that it has a 5-year warranty (like any Chrysler product). It should run me about $2000 but it will be economical and easy to keep up. I also like those Volkswagens though. Some guys are putting their orders in for Corvettes, Jaguars, and Austin-Healy's. But the only thing is some of those are foreign makes and it will be costly to keep up on repairs.

Well about me extending, there is only one job or type of job I would extend for. Either they put me working in Saigon, in the office, or what I really would like is to get into this program in the First Division which is devoted to civil action. You go into villages and towns and throw parties for the children, teach the people how to improve themselves and try to make their lives better. I tell you one thing, I don't want to spend my time out on the lines, getting sick or catching some kind of disease. It isn't worth it. But if they would give me what I want, I'll stay here for the rest of my time in the Army. If not, they can stick it up their rump.

It is really depressing to see how these mountain people live. They are called Montagnards. I bought a nifty crossbow of a "mountain man" for 100 piasters (Vietnamese money). You should see it. When you go through their villages the people are almost naked (like the people you see in Africa in National Geographic magazine).

The filth is unbelievable. They have no sewage system and they go to the toilet in the street. The water they drink isn't fit to wash your boots off with. The cattle and livestock live right with them. The funny thing about these people is that they build their houses on stilts. They live in the most primitive way. You think you moved into the prehistoric times once you walked into one of their villages.

They look at you like you're some kind of strange creature. It is really weird. Well the rain is starting again so I'd better close. Tell everyone I said hello. And you asked me in your last letter about how we move to different places. Most of the time it is by flying box cars (Dad would know what they are) and sometimes by huge helicopters called Chinooks.

Take care and don't worry.

Love,

Jack

QUAN LOI RUBBER PLANTATION AND PROCESSING

Quan Loi Area Rich In Rubber

MORE CIVIC ACTION BY THE BIG RED ONE IN VIETNAM

Balloons and rice are just two of the "other weapons" the Division uses to combat communism in South Vietnam

Instant happiness for these Vietnamese youngsters is Captain George A. Garrity passing out packets of candy and toys

September 1967

Dear Mom and Dad,

I'm sorry that I put the wrong address on those letters. I did it unconsciously.

Well I definitely decided not to put in for a helicopter gunner. I saw another helicopter get knocked down. This time the VC didn't do it. There was a malfunction on the helicopter and the thing crashed into a barracks. We were eating chow and I came out of the mess hall and suddenly, a helicopter which was just beginning to take off, began to sputter and pop. Then all at once we heard a pop and the darn propeller went one way and the tail section went another and the main body with the pilot, copilot, and three passengers went zooming for the ground. The bad thing was the two gunners on the sides tried to jump (or was blown out) and jumped from around a hundred feet up. You could hear one big scream then the copter hit. Billows of smoke came after the explosion. This only happened around 50 yards away from our area. We raced over to the crash but there wasn't much we could do. The copter and its' passengers were almost disintegrated in the flames. There were 5 killed inside the building and I saw one of the helicopter gunners. It was sickening. You could imagine what a person would look like from a hundred-foot drop, landing on the ground. The funny thing about it is the other gunner was alive, but they said almost every bone in his body was broken. I don't think he'll live.

The odds on something happening like that is one in every 16000 flights but that's too risky. Up north it's about 1 in every 6 or 7 thousand and with my luck I'd get sent up north. So, I think I'll just stay in the field I'm in, but I would like to extend, but in something less risky (perhaps Saigon security). I don't know. It's not worth all the money in the world if you don't live or get injured so you can't spend it.

About me dating these girls. Never fear, you don't have to worry about that. Most of them dislike me because I wouldn't give them the time of day. Most of these guys go wild over them, but really, they're really the most filthy and ignorant people you ever want to meet. I don't give them anything except to tell them to get the hell away. Now for the kids, I always get chewing gum and smiles. They're one of the things that help you get your mind off things. They're left on their own for most of the day and most of the GI's don't even bother to bend over and say hello. They come over and you teach them American words and the remarkable thing is that they are fairly smart, and you can have them almost talking American to you. You wouldn't believe this but most of the children, once they reach the age of walking, are smoking cigarettes.

I'm sorry this letter was written out in the field. I can't say where, but it was wet, and the letter got wet too. The good thing is that we got 4 VC. They were surprised when we came upon them and we killed them.

Well it's raining again so I better go.

Love,

Jack

Finding the Enemy

September 1967

Dear Mom and Dad,

I'm sorry about the condition of that last letter but I went out to the field for a week and it rained the whole time. Yes, I'm what you call a line journalist. I go out on-line with the infantry and send in reports and pictures to the headquarters. That's all I can say, but you may say my job is just like an infantryman because I go out every time they do, and I fire too when we get hit.

I'm attached to the 1ˢᵗ 18ᵗʰ Infantry, the nickname for them is the "Swamp Rats". It is a very good outfit. I don't know how long I'll be here or if I'll ever change. It sees a lot of action. Like we went out for a week and killed 4 VC, found 2 base camps, and found many tunnel complexes. I like it pretty much out in the field. We got mortared a few times and I tell you're glad to lay in the bottom of that hole (filled with water) and listen to those mortar rounds explode around you.

Now I'm back at Di An. They said we might be heading up to Da Nang around the Virgin Mountains, but I don't care. I talked to the extension officer about going another 6 months and he said that they give you $1800 and pay you double combat pay. I don't know exactly what field I want to extend to, but I can't extend until I'm over here for 6 months.

I'm sending home a few little items. Like the safe conduct pass (Choi hoi) which states that any VC can come up to any allied soldier and if he has this pass you can't shoot him because he is turning himself in. How did you like those elections? I figured Ky would have gotten killed, but he didn't. There was a lot of VC terrorism, but it didn't affect us too much. They only got 3 mortar rounds that were even close to us. They've been dropping a lot of napalm and having a good amount of air strikes a few miles away. Also, I'm sending a few pictures of VC type tunnels, booby traps, and Viet-namese maps. I'd send some things home, but the postage situation is terrible. They charge you so much to send a small package, I'm just waiting to send a large package home instead of a few small ones. Tell everyone I said hello. I've got an appointment.

Love,

Jack

Finding the Enemy

September 1967

Dear Mom and Dad,

Well I'm back out again in the field. We left Quan Loi yesterday and we are now somewhere on Highway 13, clearing the road for convoys. It's very hectic and tiresome. All you do is check the road out for mines and booby traps. All we've found so far is one anti-tank mine.

How's things going for you? I hope well.

Well R&R is coming up. I'm supposed to go to Australia sometime in December or January. Here's some good news, I hope. They said they cancelled our rest at Thanksgiving so we could have Christmas in the rear. I really don't believe it until I see it.

After here (we will stay here 10 days) we'll go to Lai Khe for a 1-day rest, then out to War Zone C, then to War Zone D. This will take us until Christmas time and then I hope we go back to Di An.

Well I have an ambush tonight and I guess I'll freeze my rump off. That's the funny thing. It gets 105 degrees in the day and then your blood thins out so then at night it drops to 75 or 80 and you freeze. What a way to live.

How's the weather now? Cold I bet. I hate cold worse than heat.

How's everything with the house?

Are Jerri, Jeff and Jim doing well in school? I hope so. Tell Dad to play it cool and take it easy. Tell Judy to be good.

Well I better be going. I'm going to take a bath in a mountain stream. It's so cold, man. Don't worry and take care.

Love,
Jack

P.S. I'm sending another article about us. I'll write soon.

REST AND RECUPERATION (R&R)

Waikiki Beach and Diamond Head, Hawaii
Photo by Maj R. L. Verdejo, USAF

R&R DESTINATIONS FOR THE VIETNAM SOLDIER

IT IS A WELL-KNOWN AXIOM that the rested man performs the best job. Even the knights of old and the warriors of Genghis Khan needed brief periods of rest and recuperation before returning to the rigors of the battlefield.

The 1st Infantry Division currently receives out of-country R & R quotas to Hong Kong, Bangkok, Taipei, Manila, Tokyo, Singapore, Penang, Kuala Lumpur, Hawaii and Australia. BIG RED ONE soldiers are authorized one out-of-country R & R and one seven-day leave. Personal achievement often wins a man a three-day pass (in-country R & R) to Vung Tau, a beach resort about 40 miles southeast of Saigon.

HAWAII

Most sought-after among the R & R cities are Honolulu and Sydney, but both require early application due to their popularity. HAWAII'S popularity is evident in that soldiers on R & R can visit with their families while enjoying the facilities of one of the world's most beautiful resorts. Fort DeRussy, Hawaii's R & R center, offers a limited number of accommodations on Waikiki Beach. Enlisted rates are $2 for singles and $4 for doubles, while officer rates are $2.50 and $5 respectively. Beach cabins at Bellows Air Force Base, located approximately 25 miles from Honolulu, range from $3.50 to $7 per day according to type of cabin and military grade. An R & R hotel reservation office is manned 24 hours a day at Fort DeRussy.

SYDNEY

Courtesy, friendliness and the English-speaking ability of its people make an AUSTRALIAN R&R

very attractive. Sydney, a metropolis of almost three million people, has 32 beaches, a moderate climate, skiing facilities and plenty of hospitality, a key word in the Australian vocabulary. Everything "Yank" is in vogue in the land "Down Under." "Come on 'Yank, let's have a 'pawty,' is a standard call to arms.

The R & R Center in the Chevron Hotel. Many hotels are under $10 per night. The government adopted dollars and cents currency (although the Australian dollar is worth slightly more than the American dollar).

Sydney has plenty of taxis and tipping to the nearest 10 cents is customary. Most exclusive restaurants expect a 10 to 15 per cent tip. It is recommended that you bring at least $250 for an R & R in Australia, and applications should be submitted early.

TOKYO

Tokyo's R & R center is located at Camp Zama. For $11.60, the center offers room, board, hot meals, maid service, 10 cold beers a day, one shave and a haircut, a Japanese bath and massage. Room prices run approximately $10 per night. The monetary exchange in Japan is 360 yen to one US dollar. Tipping is not necessary anywhere. Transportation is inexpensive. It is recommended you bring at least $300 for a Tokyo R & R.

HONG KONG

Hotel prices average $10 per night. The currency is the Hong Kong dollar and one US dollar is equal to HK$5.75. Taxi fares are HK$1 for the first mile and 20 cents for every fifth of a mile thereafter. Rickshaws are also available for a minimum fare of 50 cents. Tipping should be done on a 10 per cent basis.

TAIWAN

The R & R Center is in TAIPEI, the capital of Taiwan. Hotel prices range from $3 to $8 per night for a single room with a 10 per cent service charge added.

A shy Taiwanese lass

Currency in Taiwan is the National Taiwan dollar. The current rate of exchange is NT$40 to one US dollar. Rates are NT$6 for the first mile and NT$2 for each additional one-third mile.

BANGKOK

Hotel rates range from $6 to $18 per night for a single room. The basic unit of Thai currency is the baht, about equal to the American nickel. The current rate is 20.62 baht for one US dollar. Taxis operate on a bargaining basis with a

minimum fare of five baht. The average fare is 7-10 baht. For an R & R to Bangkok it is recommended that you bring at least $150.

SINGAPORE

Hotel rates vary from $6.50 to $26 for a single room. Currency in Singapore is the Malaysian dollar, equal to about 33 US cents. Metered taxis are available day or night at 40 Malaysian cents for the first mile and 20 cents for each additional half-mile. Prices increase 50 per cent after 1 a.m.

MANILA

Special R & R rates are in effect at certain hotels and average around $6 per night. Chauffeur-driven cars are for hire for $2 an hour. The currency in the Philippines is the peso with a rate of ex-

Festival time in the Philippines

change of 3.90 pesos per US dollar. A suggested amount for a Manila R & R is $200. It is advisable to bring cigarettes and health and comfort items rather than buy them in Manila. For example, cigarettes in Manila are nearly five times as costly as in a Vietnam PX.

KUALA LUMPUR

The R & R center in Kuala Lumpur is at the Merlin Hotel and in Penang at the International Hotel. The currency is the Malaysian dollar and, as in Singapore, hotel rooms range in price from $6.50 to $26 per day. Taxis in both cities are plentiful and rates are inexpensive.

VUNG TAU

The Vietnamese coastal city of VUNG TAU boasts some of the finest beaches on the South China Sea. An opportunity for an in-country R & R to this famous beach resort should not

be passed up. Your three-day pass begins as soon as you check into the R & R Center and ends on the morning of the fourth day.

The Vung Tau R & R Center features nightly band entertainment plus a PX, snack bar, library, game room and nightly movies. Free rooms are available at the center and free bus transportation will take you to the marketplace, USO or beach. Other types of transportation include the Lambretta and the horse and buggy. All shopping is done on a bargaining basis.

No matter what your choice for an R & R, there are certain criteria that must be kept in mind. Before you make your final plans, be sure you have a definite R & R allocation, your shot record is up to date, and you have your R & R orders. Most important of all is money—be sure you have enough! [8]

Penang's Captain Kling Mosque

Captain Kling Mosque, Penang, Malaysia

HIGHWAY 13 BETWEEN SAIGON AND QUAN LOI

LIFELINE. Highway 13 is the 1st Infantry Division's main supply route between Saigon and Quan Loi. BIG RED ONE control of the now famous road was won after many hard fought battles with communist forces.

(U.S. Army photo)

28

September 1967

Dear Mom and Dad,

Well I'm writing just to tell you I'm doing fine and am still on Highway 13 doing road clearance. We should be here until the end of the month then we should move to Lai Khe for a couple days rest. We got hit the other night and killed 57 of the jokers. I guess they'll never learn.

We got two new boys in yesterday. They're as green as grass. But two is better than none. Malaria has gotten quite a few of the men. I hope we get a few more in. Like I said before, we're scheduled to go to Lai Khe for a couple of days. They are supposed to award us the medals we won at Loc Ninh. When and if I get the medal, I'll send it home. After Lai Khe we go back to War Zone C then to War Zone D. D is worse than C because the jungle is worse in D. In D you can't even walk through the jungle besides seeing in it.

I'm sending a few more little clippings from the papers about us. One is about Loc Ninh and the other is about Song Be when we got mortared. This weather over here is getting pretty hot. The average in the day is 100 degrees. The problems arise when the night falls and it drops to 70 or 80 degrees and you freeze. They say your blood thins out and causes this.

That boy who got hit by that RPG round is from Cincinnati. They say it shattered his arm and he is now in Japan and will be in the states by Christmas. I'm glad in a way since the only place he wanted to go is the Conservatory of Music to study piano.

I'm hoping Australia comes up for R&R because I would like to take it. How are things going for you? Fine, I hope. I got all that gum and Kool-Aid you've been sending, and I appreciate it. That's a good way to do it. I better be going but tell everyone hello.

Love,

Jack

OPERATION GIANT SWATH

THE JUNGLES OF VIETNAM are effective obstacles to allied pacification and counterinsurgency operations. They provide the adversary with sanctuaries which are difficult to detect by aerial reconnaissance and even more difficult to reach and destroy on the ground. The 1st Infantry Division has met this challenge with a new approach to land clearing.

With the arrival in Vietnam of the 168th Land Clearing Team (LCT) in May 1967, the Rome plow came to Vietnam. A specially designed cutting blade fitted to a standard tractor, the Rome plow has since been employed in teams to completely level extensive jungles. Such well known enemy havens as the Ong Dong Jungle, the Iron Triangle, and the Hobo and Fil Hoi Woods have been literally erased from the III Corps Tactical Zone.

Operation Giant Swath, conducted by the 1st Infantry Division during May and June 1968, was conceived as a radically new approach to land clearing team employment. This operation was designed to make more effective use of the Rome plow by clearing traces along roads and trails rather than entire jungle masses, as was done in past clearing projects. A series of swaths 200 to 1000 meters wide were sliced through the jungle sanctuaries, subdividing them into small tracts bounded on all sides by either clearings, swamps or streams.

The swaths formed a continuous landing zone which permitted air assaults at any location of the tactical commander's choosing. The result was the creation of several small areas which are vulnerable to company sized reconnaissance-in-force operations. These areas thus became untenable as sites for enemy base camps and resupply installations. In addition, the detection of enemy movement was greatly facilitated.

Although the land clearing teams and engineer work forces were subjected to harassment from mines, snipers, and occasional rocket propelled grenades, the Viet Cong did not mount major resistance until almost thirty days after the operation began. By then it was too late, for the Division was already deep into enemy territory. By judicious use of forces, the BIG RED ONE was able to smash the enemy's thrusts in the south while simultaneously penetrating his base camps in the north.

The Giant Swath concept, which allowed for a rapid thrust into the heart of enemy territory before the enemy had an opportunity to react, proved highly successful. The measurable results of the operation were 11,000 acres of enemy jungle destroyed, 60 kilometers of road built or upgraded, six major base camps destroyed, and numerous supply caches uncovered. In addition, the rocket attacks on Lai Khe were reduced to one-fourth the intensity experienced prior to the operation.

Statistics are always impressive, but a true measure of the success of Giant Swath will become more apparent in the months to come. The military and political advantages gained by the effective denial of 200 square kilometers of enemy territory by the selective clearing of one-fourth of the area, as well as the opening of two major routes into the previously isolated Michelin Rubber Plantation, are certain to change the entire conduct of the war in the Giant Swath operational zone. The 1st Infantry Division has added yet another chapter to its proud history by conceiving and proving a significant tactical innovation in the Vietnam War.[9]

OPERATION GIANT SWATH

DEEP CUTS such as these greatly reduce enemy infiltration and ambush opportunities.

LONG RANGE RECONNAISSANCE

CHAPTER FIVE
OCTOBER-NOVEMBER 1967

INTENSE FIGHTING AND A SILVER STAR

In the fall of 1967, Jack had been in Vietnam about 3 months and he began October with a rest before several months of intense fighting.

He volunteered for the First Division Long Range Reconnaissance team since he wanted more action. Jack proudly earned his Combat Infantry badge and was promoted to Specialist-4, with a pay increase, making $250 per month. He completed Jump School since he wanted to be Ranger qualified and perhaps ultimately become a Green Beret.

Along with valiantly fighting the Viet Cong, Jack battled leech infestations, claiming some were as long as garter snakes he saw back home, filth, and exhaustion. He was amazed by the wealth of food available in the jungle and got his first taste of python. Jack appreciated some mortar attacks since they kept the enemy away and allowed him to sleep.

Jack valued his Army fighting experience since it had "grown him up" and caused him to forgo "sin" he would have otherwise committed if he was home. I recall we were a pretty religious family growing up. Jack attended Catholic school and church regularly, so 'sinning' was supposed to be avoided. Thus, he undoubtedly had moral anxieties regarding his wartime behavior especially what his unit did to enemy soldiers after killing them although it was considered on par with what the enemy did to dead US soldiers. He also acknowledged that he matured because of his service, realizing he would not have otherwise.

Jack described getting shot but not wounded then not realizing he got hit by shrapnel, earning his first Purple Heart. He was involved in brutal combat near Loc Ninh in the Battle of Srok Silamlite III where his valor earned him a Silver Star, then a Bronze Star the following day for killing a sniper. He had a 'traditional' Thanksgiving meal, cleaned his rifle after eating and ended November 1967 doing road clearance on Highway 13 (Thunder Road), knowing there were more battles to come.

October 1, 1967

Dear Mom and Dad,

Well I've moved again. I'm now at Phuoc Vinh around 30 miles northwest of Saigon. I can't say how long we'll be here. It's like a 3 to 10-day rest. We probably go into War Zone C after this.

Well I did something that you will probably call stupid. I put in for the First Division Long Range Reconnaissance team. I probably go to jump school because you have to be airborne in around two weeks. You are Ranger qualified and you are sent in 5-man teams and their jobs are to recon and look for any traces of VC before any unit of the Division moves in. You probably think it's dangerous. The only dangerous part so far will be the airborne part, but you get used to that just by riding in those open helicopters. I think it will be very good and it's what I want to do and when you come out you have something to be proud of and the next step after this is the Green Beret boys. I don't think I have to jump out of airplanes too much, but they make you do this just in case they can't land you if the jungle gets too thick.

Well good news. I made Spec-4 at the end of this month. That means I'll be making around $250 a month but what I like about it is that if I make Spec-4 so soon, and if I play my cards right, I'll probably earn my Sergeant's stripes. I'll send you a picture when I get my eagle (the emblem you get for Specialist).

I'm looking forward to making my first jump. I don't think there will be much trouble. Well I earned my CIB (Combat Badge, a rifle with blue field and wreath around it) by having a sniper fire a few rounds at us yesterday. All we did was return fire and run like the blazes. We are expected to get mortared tonight, but I hope not. This place is like a dump. Most of the guys are coming down with VD after fooling around with those women at Quan Loi. Now they have to get shots in the rear, and they say the needle is eight inches long. They thought they'd be safe but now they're reaping the wages for their sins.

I was talking to a few guys and they said I'll probably get sent to Germany when I get back to the states because I'll have so much time left. I hope not, it gets so cold in Germany in the winter. What I'd like to do is stay here in Vietnam for the rest of my 3 years. It just doesn't seem possible that I've been here for almost 4 months. You don't have much time to rest or think.

How's things going at home? Are the kids enjoying school? How's Jerri doing at U.C. Say hello to Dad. Tell him he's going to have an airborne ranger for a son.

The artillery is now blazing away. The gun ships are taking off to rocket bomb a VC base camp or route. You should hear those jets when they drop a load of napalm. It's still raining and humid over here. Boy I'm going to hate January when the hot season gets here.

I see back in the states you're having more riots, having many hurricanes and Cincinnati finally got its' football team. The only thing they haven't got is a place to play except Crosley Field or U.C. stadium.

I'm looking out the tent side and I notice a fuel dump across the street. I hope we don't get mortared because that stuff will sure go up if a mortar hits it.

Before I forget, please call up Bill's mother and ask her for Bill's address and Paul S. address. I hate to ask you again but they both got wet when I went through a waist-high rice paddy up at Quan Loi.

I'm sure glad we got out of that leech-filled location. I'll tell you one thing that is the honest-to-God truth. I saw leeches in those rice paddies that were big as garter snakes back in the states. I had four of them in me (smaller of course). You'd be walking along, and you feel something crawling on you like a bug but the worst thing you can do is try to grab it because as soon as you touch it, it digs in. A leech looks like a snail with antennae and has a brownish color. It falls on you or when you're in water and it crawls on you. I had one on my neck, but I didn't panic. I just got someone to smack it off. You should feel it dig in. Those antennae on its head just ram themselves into the skin and you feel it. The best thing is to put mosquito repellent on it and it dissolves, head and all. Leeches are just like ticks (only twice as large). If you do get its head out, you don't accomplish anything. Some guys try to burn them out, pull them out, cut them out and all they do is probably get it infected.

The only thing with the mosquito repellent method is after you pour the juice on them, it dissolves the leech entirely and it leaves a hole in the skin and then the blood flows so hard, you think it'll never stop. I don't mind it in the jungle. It can be dangerous though if you try to fight it. There's enough to live on in the jungle for the rest of your life if you just look. There are bananas, grapefruit, coconuts, tapioca, bamboo meat (the inside of the bamboo), nuts, berries and more. All you have to do is look for it. For water, you have streams, water in bamboo, and cassava plants and many more. For meat, you have small game, birds, snakes, and monkeys. I had my first piece of monkey while I was at Quan Loi. Also, my first piece of python. The best animal for survival is a pet monkey. All you do is follow him, eat what he eats, drink what he drinks and if there isn't anything else, you have him. HA HA.

The artillery and mortars are now starting. It's music to our ears because as long as they're firing, we can go to sleep because it keeps Charlie away. Guys got a hold of some pot (marijuana) and are smoking. They act just like kids. I can't see how anybody can act like children to get drunk and take drugs. That's one thing the Army has taught me. It showed me how foolish and childish I was. If I was back in civilian life, I know I would join the club and drink and smoke dope, but the Army has "grown me up." Only the children haven't grown up and these are fools who will get themselves killed. The sorry part of it is that it will probably get a buddy killed. It's now raining again, and the wind is blowing. I best be going, it's now 8:45 (18:45 hours) Oct. 1ˢᵗ and it's pitch dark outside. So please don't worry. I'll be fine. Take care.

Love,

Jack

P.S, I sent 30 dollars home in a money order. I also have $350 in the Soldiers deposit, so you don't have to worry about me spending too much money.

Special Forces action

U.S. MARSHALS AND THE PENTAGON RIOT OF OCTOBER 21, 1967

The October 1967 Pentagon riot, the first national protest against the war, exemplified the agonizingly divisive debate over Vietnam. Ironically, the demonstrators helped the federal government confirm its own commitment to civilian control. Civilian Deputy Marshals, not soldiers, arrested them. The Deputies were fulfilling the historic role of U.S. Marshals, for each arrest affirmed the enduring concept of civilian supremacy in the United States.

The riot lasted the night. The Deputy Marshals, acting as the civil authority of the federal government, made all the arrests. As soon as they were arrested, many of the demonstrators simply collapsed, forcing the Deputies to drag them to the waiting prison vans where other Deputies pushed and shoved the recalcitrant demonstrators aboard. The Deputies worked without relief, taking few breaks. Physically exhausted, they responded to the rioters with increasingly rough treatment, though remarkably few injuries. A total of 682 people were arrested. Forty-seven people-demonstrators, soldiers, and U.S. Marshals were injured. By 7:00 o'clock Sunday morning, most of the protestors had left; only 200 remained.

SATURDAY, 5:40 P.M.
DEMONSTRATORS MARCH TO PENTAGON:

The day's activities began with a rally at the Lincoln Memorial. Fifty thousand protestors, "armed with limp flowers and sturdy convictions," gathered to protest the war. After 3:00 p.m., some demonstrators headed for home. Others headed toward the Pentagon for more rallies.

SATURDAY, 6:00 P.M.-
DEMONSTRATORS STORM PENTAGON

Some of the demonstrators were determined to disrupt military operations by storming the Pentagon. The most serious incident occurred when 20 to 30 demonstrators pushed

through the line of U.S. Marshals and military police into the Pentagon's Mall entrance. They were greeted by heavily armed troops. The soldiers forced some demonstrators outside. Others were carried out bodily.[10]

SHENANDOAH II

September-December 1967

REGARDLESS OF THE TIME, the place or even the individual people involved, there always will be one combat operation in Vietnam that stands above the rest in terms of unit achievement—the big operation—the one veterans, war correspondents and students of military history will remember best. Such an operation is SHENANDOAH II, launched by Major General John H. Hay, on 29 Sept 1967.

Early in September, General Hay set in motion an elaborate plan for the concentration of psychological operations (PSYOPS) along Highway 13. Area studies had indicated that the major proportion of the population in the Division's Tactical Area of Interest (TAOI) were concentrated on or near that road and economically concerned with it. PSYOPS leaflets were being dropped by the Division on villages all the way from Lai Thieu to Loc Ninh.

Other plans had been in progress during this time also, principally the permanent removal of Division Headquarters, Danger Main, from Di An northward to Lai Khe, home of the 3d Brigade, where, as Danger Forward, it had been situated for previous operations. The move was accomplished in September, concurrent with discussions to also displace the 1st Brigade from Phuoc Vinh northward to the An Loc/Quan Loi area.

Division Headquarters never returned to Di An. And before Operation SHENANDOAH II was to terminate, the 1st Brigade would relocate to Quan Loi. Thus, the entire Division headquarters and logistical apparatus was astride Highway 13 by 30 October.

The BIG RED ONE'S mission was to destroy the 271st and other enemy units in the area and to clear as much jungle within the time frame of the operation as available resources permitted.

Within two days, after the battalion, minus B Company, had conducted a reconnaissance-in-force mission without incident, the Battle of Da Yeu would erupt.

DA YEU

At 1500 hours on 6 October 1967, the "Swamp Rats" received live 60mm mortar rounds in their NDP. The NDP was in a natural clearing with the tree line about 20 meters from the northern sector and 75 to 100 meters from the other sectors.

In addition to establishing listening posts (LPS), each company sent out an ambush patrol. Rain was relentless.

The Viet Cong stayed within the tree line during their attacks and were not visible except when they ignited trip flares that the 1st Battalion, 18th Infantry, had planted among the trees. Claymores either in the trees or in the clearing near the tree line were detonated by the Big Red One infantryman from their bunkers. Many of the mines were replaced by men who crawled outside the perimeter during lulls in the fighting. According to the rallier, - who remained in the enemy basecamp during the attack, his unit lost 59 killed and 67 wounded in the Battle of Da Yeu in addition to 20 killed by a B-52 strike on 14 October. US losses for the action amounted to two killed and eight wounded.

FOUR DAYS LATER, on 11 October, the 1/18 Infantry departed its NDP and headed north on a battalion-size patrol into the south Chon Thanh Sector of Binh Long Province. It was a single column consisting of B Company, the command group and C Company.[11]

October 13, 1967

Dear Mom and Dad

Well I'm enjoying what I'm doing now. I've completed jump school. I am in the field at Phuoc Vinh and I tell you I've already seen enough action that I'll ever want to see. The first day we were there, we dug in. Thank God they didn't hit us that night because we were digging in until 1:00 in the morning. Then we have guard at least three hours a night so we get around three hours a night to sleep. I tell you one thing I've never been so tired as I have been now.

Things are so bad here we can't even get 150 meters outside the perimeter without getting hit. Our battalion, since we've been here, have lost 5 men. The 1ˢᵗ of the 2ⁿᵈ Infantry (who we relieved lost 42). We got hit the second night and bullets were flying all over the place. Shrapnel was also thick. After that night we had 19 VC killed in the battalion and our company killed 16 of them. CBS TV reporters were doing a report on us and I heard their report consisted of our brutality to the dead VC. You see in the 1ˢᵗ Infantry Division after you kill a VC you chop off his ears and stick a Red One patch in his mouth. They thought it was pretty brutal. It is until you see what they do to our guys after they get us. The radio operator for an ambush on Bravo Company was killed by a Claymore mine and they had to leave his body to get the rest to safety. We found the body the next day with his body slashed up and his body and radio and weapon, booby trapped.

I thought I had it yesterday when we went out on patrol. The day before Charlie Company got hit in the exact same place and lost two men. I never was so scared in all my life. We went into the wood line and we were on the point. First, we got sniper fire on the left in a tree. We all got down, then sniper fire on the right. I was so confused; I fired my M-14 AR with a grenade launcher, and I think I killed the joker on the right but after we returned fire. The front was hit with automatic fire and I thought it was all over. Bullets were zipping all around. I thought I got hit once but the bullet grazed the ammunition magazine on my hip (that's my first souvenir). We pulled out, but fast. Two guys got it in the back but not too seriously.

The General said we were the last brigade. That's 4 battalions. There are an estimated 2 VC regiments in the area. About those dead VC, I did the most sickening thing in my life. I buried three of those earless VC dead bodies. Rigor mortis had set in and they were stiff as a board. So, joker kept hitting one of them with a shovel. We had to drag them over to the hole and then we kicked them in. It's almost unreal.

Flash! We just got the word; we're going back to Di An for a three-day rest. I'm glad everybody is exhausted and jumpy. They don't give you enough to feed a bird. We get a doughnut for breakfast.

I tell you the two most scary things we have to do. Ambushes and LP (listening posts). Both are done at night and Charlie is looking for you just as hard as you are looking for them. For LP, you sit just outside the perimeter and listen for movement. You're in danger more from your own men than Charlie. You can't see a thing and they're all over the place.

Those mortar attacks are something else. We had two hundred of those things come down on us and not one came near me. Well I've told too many war stories already.

For that package, I wouldn't send anything. I don't need anything. Anyway, I will be out in the jungle at Christmas time and most likely I wouldn't get it so I wouldn't send it but thanks anyway. For Pete's sake, whatever you do, don't worry. I enjoy what I'm doing. I can take care of myself. How's everything been going? I've been getting your letters regularly and I really enjoy them. My promotion is coming out pretty soon. At least I hope so. How's everyone doing in school? Is Jerri doing well? Is Jeff and Jim doing well? Tell Judy to be good. If the car takes too much money to repair, take it out of the bank. tell Dad I said hello and tell him I'm in a darn good outfit.

If Bill calls up, tell him sorry but I'm lucky to get a letter off to you.
Well I've got to get some sleep now.

Love,

Jack

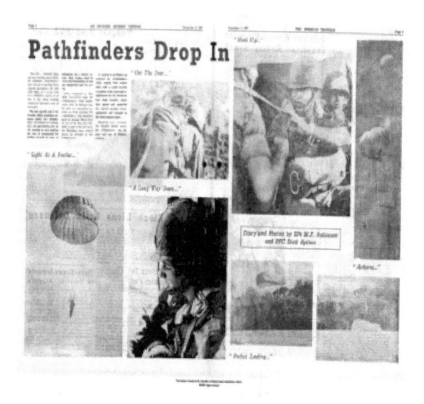

RECONNAISSANCE

ONG THANH

The next big contact with the 271st occurred on 17 October 1967 in the BATTLE OF ONG THANH, some 12 miles northeast of Lai Khe.

The following morning the battlefield was cleared of the dead. The BATTLE OF ONG THANH had cost the 271st VC Regiment 163 men by body count, many of them victims of deadly artillery fire and airstrikes. US losses were 53 killed and 58 wounded.

Shortly after midnight on 29 October, compounds at Loc Ninh began receiving heavy mortar fire, which was the beginning of one of the greatest battles of the Vietnam War. Less than an hour later, reports started filtering into the Division's tactical operations center (DTOC) that elements of the 273rd VC Regiment were massing for a ground attack against these remote outposts, 40 miles north of Lai Khe. By 0300 hours, the defenders had succeeded in repulsing this first assault. Phase II of Operation SHENANDOAH II had begun.

SROK SILAMLITE I

SHORTLY PRIOR TO NOON on October 29, 1967, an urgent request for assistance came from a Special Forces/CIDG element.

Moving north through the rubber trees, the company contacted the North Vietnamese approximately 600 meters from its NDP. The 1st Platoon immediately engaged the NVA unit with squads advancing in the bounding overwatch method and overran the enemy position, killing nine.

Enemy losses in the BATTLE OF SROK SILAMLITE I were 24 killed. US casualties were one killed and nine wounded.

SROK SILAMLITE II

THE FOLLOWING MORNING, 30 October 1967, A Company of the 1/18 Infantry contacted an estimated battalion of the 165th Regt south of the "Dogface" NDP.

At 1230 hours, as the company moved up the hill, the point element saw an enemy soldier stand up on the finger of the slope and engaged him with small arms fire immediately, fire was returned by the NVA force and the BATTLE OF SROK SI-LAMLITE II began.

As the BIG RED ONE soldiers moved up the hill, an enemy machinegun in a bunker opened fire. Specialist 4 Ronald L. Campsey, **PRIVATE FIRST-CLASS JOHN D. FREP-PON** and Private First-Class Joseph F. Hayman spotted the emplacement and with their comrades providing covering fire, began to maneuver against it. Nearing the complex, they were taken under fire by the enemy, but succeeded in overrunning it and killing the three North Vietnamese inside, thus enabling the remainder of the company to advance unimpeded. All three men were awarded the Silver Star Medal for their actions during this battle. Seven enemy trenches were overrun, putting the NVA soldiers in full flight to the southwest through a draw.

Enemy losses in SROK SILAMLITE II were 83 killed whereas, US casualties were only four killed and five wounded.

LOC NINH AIRSTRIP

AT 0055 HOURS ON 31 OCTOBER 1967, the fire support patrol base at the airstrip and the Special Forces/CIDG camp were again mortared.

THE FIRST DAY OF NOVEMBER saw a slackening in the bitter fighting, as enemy fire, while directed at all friendly positions around Loc Ninh, was only light and sporadic.

The BIG RED ONE conducted a Medical Civic Action Program (MEDCAP) in the village of Loc Ninh itself, treating 75 patients while the Division Band held a concert in the village square. Twenty cases of blankets and 1,500 pounds of rice were also distributed to Loc Ninh refugees, several thousand of whom had journeyed to An Loc, 13 miles south when the fighting broke out on 29 October.

SROK SILAMLITE III

AT 0030 HOURS ON 2 NOVEMBER 1967, the 1/18 Infantry NDP came under a heavy mortar attack which lasted approximately 20 minutes.

Patrols ran into the perimeter yelling "ambush" to warn the occupants of the impending ground attack from the south. Running behind the last man also yelling "ambush" was a Viet Cong, whom the guard at the entrance to the NDP spotted and killed.

This two-hour period was one of the most colorful of the war. From their NDP, the "Swamp Rats" saw the sky alternately illuminated by flares, artillery and mortar shells, rockets and bombs. The downward parabolas of red tracers from the supporting gunships were matched by those curving upward from the enemy's heavy machine-guns. And far from ceasing when airstrikes were brought in, the enemy gunners let go with bursts of fire at the low swooping jets.

Initial losses for the enemy, later identified as elements of the 273rd VC Regt, were 220 killed, but as search and destroy missions continued for the next five days, additional bodies were found in the area until the mounting toll reached 263. US losses in the superb NDP fortification were only one killed and eight wounded.

BU NHO RUNG

JUST AFTER MIDNIGHT, the morning of 3 November 1967, a man with a flashlight entered the NDP of the 2nd Battalion, 12th Inf. A sergeant yelled, "Douse that light!" before realizing that a VC squad had inadvertently entered the position. Mortars fired from the north preceded a ground attack commencing at 0230 hours from the northeast.

AFTER THE BATTLE OF BU NHO RUNG, the village of Loc Ninh grew quiet again and its inhabitants poured homeward from An Loc. Nevertheless, the Division remained vigilant and continued to conduct search and destroy missions throughout the area, killing 41 more Viet Cong in scattered actions.

SROK RUNG

ON 7 NOVEMBER 1967 FIGHTING FLARED ANEW as the 1st Bn, 26th Inf, caught an estimated VC battalion in a sweep 5 miles northeast of Loc Ninh, called the BATTLE OF SROK RUNG.

A sweep of the battlefield turned up 66 VC bodies, while another 27 enemy had been killed by air support. US losses were 18 killed and 20 wounded.

Also waging its own particular brand of warfare in SHENANDOAH II was the Division's G-5 staff section, through psychological operations and civil affairs. Here, the BIG RED ONE assisted by providing rice, oats, wheat, canned milk and portable latrines. PSYOPS activities took place during most of the operation and centered about leaflet drops and loudspeaker broadcasts. During a six-week period a total of 5,875,000 leaflets were dropped in support of combat operations.

OPERATION SHENANDOAH II TERMINATED. ON 19 NOVEMBER 1967, after 51 days which included some of the most vicious fighting any division has engaged in since coming to Vietnam. During this time 1st Inf Division units involved in the operation accounted for 993 Viet Cong killed by body count.

Captured were 70 individual and 30 crew-served weapons, 250 tons of rice, 27 tons of salt, and huge amounts of ammunition, equipment, supplies, documents and clothing. Destroyed were 1,994 bunkers and structures.

A total of 2,234 sorties were flown, more than 2,776 tons of ordnance expended, and 23 B-52 strikes conducted. Artillery ammunition consumed amounted to 142,264 rounds.

THE HIGHLIGHT OF SHENANDOAH II was, of course, the battle for Loc Ninh.

On 5 November after a combined total of nearly 1,000 enemy soldiers had been killed at Loc Ninh by US and ARVN units, General Hay escorted the press through the "Dogface" NDP.

Months later, General Hay reflected that Loc Ninh—one of the greatest battles and most lop-sided victories of the war—

was the result of a tremendously professional job on the part of every soldier, staff officer and subordinate commander. "The single fault was that the teamwork and skill of the BIG RED ONE made it look too easy!"[12]

Operation Shenandoah II

OPERATION SHENANDOAH II

THE "DOGFACE" NDP was the scene of vicious fighting wherein 59 Viet Cong were killed on 6 October 1965

"SWAMP RATS" from the 1st Battalion, 18th Infantry, prepare night defensive positions near Bo Vou.

OPERATION SHENANDOAH II
NEWSPAPERS SENT HOME BY JACK

November 9, 1967

Dear Mom and Dad,

I have to apologize for not writing in so long a time, but this is a lot different than my other job.

This is the first "rest" we've had in two months; Time is really going fast over here, and I must admit we've been in a lot of action. We have been in 4 fire fights (battles) and killed around (and this is not an exaggeration) 1000 gooks. At Shenandoah Operation we wiped out 200 of those pigs. We lost around 5 men which was the bad thing.

The 1st Infantry Division is seeing the most action since the beginning of the war. The only thing, the rest of the battalions don't have their stuff together and I have to say, the VC are getting the best out of them. I can't say what units but last month one battalion was whipped so badly then the man who was in charge of the battalion, after the battle was a Sergeant. The battalion commander was killed, all the Captains, Lieutenants, and Sergeants E-6 and above. Just 3 days ago another unit was hit. They lost 66 men and a battalion commander. The funny thing about the VC these days is that they stay there and fight you instead of running away.

We were on Dogface Hill, 3000 meters from Loc Ninh (where the VC overran last week) and I didn't think we'd make it out of there. They tried to overrun us, that's where they made their first mistake. There were bodies lying around all over the place. We got 2 wounded VC and they said that they were told to take the hill at any cost. The actual body count that we got that night was 400. They smelled so bad you could hardly stand it. Some of them were shot and blown up. It was hard to realize they were human beings.

The next day we went on a patrol and man did we get hit. I was shaking so bad I could hardly stand up. The funny thing about it was I killed 5 VC and the battalion commander saw me and he put me in for a Silver Star. It sounds ridiculous that he put me in, but he said I risked my life. I was so scared I didn't even know I got hit with some shrapnel. Not bad, just in the face and the wrist. I'm fine though now. Not bragging but I'm going to feel funny coming home with all those medals and junk. I hope we don't have to fight any more.

About going north, that place we went to last was 65 miles north west of Saigon and 5 miles east of the Cambodian border. We wiped out almost 2 regiments of VC. I hope that was the last action that we've seen but I don't believe so. We still have Christmas to go through and that's another bad time. That boy I was talking about named Bill, well he was wounded pretty badly by shrapnel that night we got hit. He's going home bad they think. That's the saddest thing to see your buddy screaming with pain and crying for his mother. I don't know.

This filth over here is getting us down. The rainy season is about over and the heat is coming in. The dust is so thick sometimes you can hardly breathe. Well I'm finally making Spec-4 at the end of this month. About Christmas, you don't have to send me anything. I don't need a thing. I won't be able to send you anything until February because we won't be close to a Post Office until then.

I'm still hesitant about what to do after this year. I don't know what to do. I wouldn't mind extending or if I don't. you don't know where I'll go. To Germany? I wouldn't mind going but that's another year away. Well I have to be running now. They're having memorial services for the men who were killed on Dogface Hill. So, take care and don't worry. I'll write again tomorrow.

Love,

Jack

P.S. Tell everyone I said hello.

November 22, 1967

Dear Mom and Dad,

I received your two letters and enjoyed reading them very much. You shouldn't have gone to the trouble of making up a package but if it isn't too late, would you please put a package of gum (not for myself but for the Viet kids). They really love gum.

Things are going well again since we got out of the hot spot. I hope we never go back there. The Stars and Stripes gave us a big write-up (it is the official Army paper for Vietnam). You should have heard it. They said the 271ˢᵗ VC hardcore Regiment probed our area, under torrid rain (this part was <u>really</u> true) and tried to set up for a human wave but were repelled when we opened up on them. I tell you one thing; I never was so scared. They said we killed 25 VC. I know one thing, four of us had to bury 3 earless VC who died that night. Walter Cronkite of CBS called us "head-hunters" because we clipped off their ears and stuck Red One patches in their mouths.

The funny thing, the next day we had a reconnaissance patrol, and man they hit us with everything. I got put in for a Bronze Star because they think I killed one of their snipers. We were in the lead element and had two guys get hit when we were pulling out. Some guys were so scared they couldn't pull the triggers. We stayed there a few days and then they pulled us out for a rest. The red mud up here is terrible. You can't get it off.

Somebody sure must be pulling for us because the very day we pulled out of that hell hole the VC tried to pull another human wave and succeeded on the 1ˢᵗ Division 28ᵗʰ Infantry (who replaced us) but they must have been asleep or something and the VC overran the place killing 56 and wounding 65. You won't believe this, but the highest-ranking man left in the Battalion was a Sergeant E-6. The Colonel was killed, two Majors, all the Captains (4 in number) and all the Lieutenants, top Sergeants and Sergeants E-7. They know exactly where to strike and do the damage.

They finally pulled everyone back and are going to B-52 bomb the place. That is what they should have done in the first place. Two of the last VC battalions (these guys are fanatics and dope addicts) strap bombs and mines on their bodies and blow them if they think they can get you. Let's get off the unpleasantness of this place.

Well I'll be going in for a 15-day rest the 15th of November until the 1st of December. The only part about this is that I'll be out in the field during Christmas. In a way this will be good because the VC have their biggest terrorist actions during Christmas because GI's tend to slacken up and forget to stay alert. Out in the boonies you always stay alert because if you don't, heh, you probably won't wake up.

The worst thing over here for me is L-P (Listening Post) at night. They stick you in a spot and give you a mess of Claymore mines to set up and your job is to sit there all night and just listen for movement or noise. I was out there the night after we got hit. Man, I was shaking like a leaf. Then we blew a Claymore (because we thought we heard movement) and a piece of shrapnel set off a trip flare behind us and those nuts back in the perimeter thought it was a VC and started opening up. About 5 grenades landed around two feet behind our hole. That night I said I wasn't going to go out unless I had a hole to get into and that was the only thing that saved us. The guys laughed at me for digging it but after that they just shook my hand.

I tell you the most wonderful and awesome thing to see is those jets come in and have an air strike on VC positions. At that place we were at you couldn't go 100 meters outside the perimeter without getting hit. They said it was the worst actual fighting the 1st Division had ever been in (I'm glad now I've seen the worst so things can't get worse). Those jets would come in around 200 meters from our positions and blow the tar out of the place. Then they'd spray the area with 20-millimeter cannons. Shrapnel is flying all over the place. The funny thing, the VC just go in their holes and come out right after the attack. The only thing which will stop them are the B-52's. It's getting dark and we are not allowed to have lights, so I'll write again later. Take care and tell everyone I said hello.

Love,

Jack

P.S. Today is the anniversary of the Kennedy death.

BIG RED ONE action in Operation Shenandoah II

NIGHT WARFARE IN VIETNAM

DRY LEAVES ABOVE him glowed golden in the fading light as his men settled into their ambush positions. Captain Glade M. Bishop crouched and waited for darkness. The sound of firing to the south caused him to wonder if his feeling had been wrong. Maybe this would not be the night they would get their ambush.

Once it had been true that the Viet Cong were masters of the night. Like small armies of carnivorous ants, they moved silently through the jungles, leaving destruction as they went.

They infiltrated from the north to Saigon, gliding along rivers in sampans and marching down trails under cover of darkness. Night had been their ally.

Now, like the two platoons of men who lay silently to the left and right of the Ambush Battalion company commander, men from almost every unit of the 1st Infantry Division are using night as a means of demoralizing the enemy, striking physical and psychological blows to every VC and NVA soldier. "

Taking the night away from Charlie" is the phrase being used to denote nightly BIG RED ONE tactics against the enemy. Stated former Division commander, Major General Keith L. Ware, "Ambush patrols are the most effective weapon we have against enemy infiltration and night movement."

Because of its almost nightly contact with the enemy, the battalion's enemy body count was quickly becoming tops in the Division with a kill ratio of 320 enemy to one allied KIA.[13]

THANKSGIVING MENU

Shrimp Cocktail
With
Crackers

Roast Turkey   Turkey Gravey
Cornbread Dressing
Mashed Potatoes

Glazed Sweet Potatoes   Cranberry Sauce
Buttered
Peas or mixed vegetables
Crisp Relish Tray

Hot Rolls   Butter

Pumpkin Pie
With
Whipped Cream

Mincemeat Pie   Old Fashion Fruit Cake
Assorted Fresh Fruit
Mixed Nuts
Assorted Candy

Iced Tea With Lemon   Milk

Thanksgiving 1967 menu sent home by Jack

November 26, 1967

Dear Mom and Dad,

Just dropping a line to tell you I'm fine. Well I'm still on Highway 13 doing road clearance. We got hit again last night by an estimated battalion and we kicked their rump again. Mortars killed 3 and wounded 17 but we got close to 100 of them and many of them were officers. We are cleaning up after the battle now. Picking up bodies and documents, weapons, ammo, etc. The one thing I like about this unit is that we aren't afraid to fight Charlie anytime or place. We don't go looking for fights, but we don't run when we find them. I never thought I'd ever enjoy fighting and this kind of life but when you see a gook and you shoot at him and see him fall. That brings the deepest personal satisfaction you can have because you know that's just one less that may get you or your buddies. And another thing is that our battalion commander, Colonel C. is the best soldier and one of the best men you would ever want to have as your commander. He hates this place, but he knows he's got a job to do so he does it. Most everyone would follow him to China if he told us to go because he'll do anything in his power to get everyone through. He'll call down the world to help us in a bind. We are one of the few units who call in and get air strikes and artillery strikes anytime we're hit. That man knows his business.

What a way to spend Thanksgiving Day. We had the traditional meal (if you want to call it that). I'm sending the menu (HA HA). Did you have a nice meal like you usually do? Like I always say, no one cooks a Thanksgiving dinner like Mein Mutter. It's getting hotter every day now. Please excuse the handwriting because my hands are so sweaty and dirty. Well the engineers have finally finished laying the barbed-wire fence. Now at least we won't get human waved so easily. There goes one of those new helicopters they got now. The Huey's that are now being used will probably be replaced by it. It is so small, and the pilot sits in the back instead of the front and it shoots as fast as a Huey copter. Almost another month has passed. In December I'll be starting in the sixth month. Time does fly. How's everything doing back home? I hope well. Everyone is probably all right. I'm glad. Is Jerri doing well? How's Jeff doing? Tell Jim and Judy I said hello. Ask Dad to drop a line if he doesn't mind. How's the house and Cincinnati doing?

Those VC want 3 cease fires this year. One for Tet (New Year's), Christmas, and some other holiday. I don't trust them. Yea. Some of us will get the chance to see the Bob Hope show at Christmas but I'll believe I'll pass up the chance because it's too easy to get mortared or have a bomb planted in the seats. I soon just stay out in the field. It's safer. I hope we don't get hit tonight. Too many guys are getting hurt. Malaria is taking a large toll too. I wish they'd get us a few more replacements. A late report on last night. Flash, they found two prisoners. One of them tried to pull a grenade and throw it. But the only thing, he didn't quite make it so now there is only one prisoner. I'm sending a leaflet telling the VC to give up. There's not much more I can say because I have to clean my rifle so that's it for now. So, take care and don't worry.

Love,

Jack

CHAPTER SIX

DECEMBER 1967-MARCH 1968

TET OFFENSIVE

I only have two letters Jack wrote between Thanksgiving 1967 and April 1968. He admits it was a long time between letters but outlines a period of severe combat and frequent firefights.

He had ambush duty on Christmas eve but got to meet Bob Hope and sit up front for the Christmas USO show since he earned a Silver Star medal.

Jack's most recent desired destination where he wanted to be stationed after his Vietnam tour ended was Fort Knox but he also wrote about extending his tour, thus he was torn between staying with his comrades or going home. He indicated he would forgo R&R since he felt it cost too much and I was told describing Jack as frugal was an understatement. He worked hard and risked his life for all he earned in Vietnam.

He shared his hawkish views about the 1968 US Presidential election and how the war should be fought, predicting losing unless tactics change. Jack and his unit spent Christmas and the following week clearing Highway 13 then moved to Lai Khe, outside of Saigon.

The Vietnamese initiated the "Tet Offensive" in late January 1968. Tet or Vietnamese New Year was typically a time for a cease-fire between North Vietnam and the US forces, but the Viet Cong attacked several South Vietnamese cities when the Tet holiday began. Jack indicated it was bad and worse than reported in the US. Jack's company was assigned to protect the US Commander's headquarters (MACVI) at Tan Son Nhut air base outside Saigon during the Tet offensive as a precaution and repelled an attack with no US casualties. A Viet Cong platoon battled their way into the US Embassy complex, also in Saigon, shocking US command although the attackers were destroyed.

Jack and his comrades fought the Viet Cong during the rest of February and March, regaining lost South Vietnamese territory and cities. Even though his Vietnam tour was scheduled to end in June 1968, he indicated he would probably extend another year when they returned to the 1st Infantry Division headquarters at Di An in May to avoid being stationed in Korea (which would be too cold for him).

He indicated he would be home for a 30-day R&R in May so he had much on his mind while trying to decide on the direction for his future.

Soldiers attend a USO performance

December 25, 1967

Dear Mom & Dad,

Merry Christmas! I hope you did have a nice Christmas. It wasn't too Merry here though. I had ambush duty Christmas eve. (boy what fun). There's a one-day truce for Christmas day and so far, it hasn't been broken. I'm on Highway 13, outside Lai Khe, doing road clearance (keeping the road cleared for convoys). It's not too bad. We had a little trouble with the VC when we first got here, but lately no trouble whatsoever. We changed battalion commanders the other day. The previous colonel is going home (he is quite a fine man), and some dud is taking his place

I had a nice little present Christmas eve day. I was allowed to go to the Bob Hope show, but they stuck us way in the back. So, to my luck, they asked if any Distinguished Service Cross winners or any Silver Star winners in the audience. So, since I got the Silver Star, they told us to go behind the stage and we got to meet Bob Hope and the performers. A general was there also. Then they took us to the first two rows (which were reserved) and placed us there for the show. So maybe my Star came in handy. The show was good but today is another day. The present temperature is 102 degrees and it is hot. In January it gets up to 120 degrees.

I received your package and letters and cards. The package was very good. We also get little packages from Elks Clubs and VFW clubs. Little odds and ends. They cheated us out of our rests, and they told us it will be in June until we see Di An again. And we will be short!

We got our dream sheets the other day. Dream sheets are sheets you fill out for the place you want to be sent after Vietnam. So, I filled it out and asked for Ft. Knox. I doubt I get it and the Sergeant said RA's (regular Army) will probably get Korea (because they need veterans in Korea) and if that happens I just extend 6 months over here. I'll have 18 months after this tour and Korea is a 13-month tour. I extend 6 months this close to 2 months leave when I do get home, will leave me with about 10 months too short for a tour in Korea or Germany.

About my money. You know "old Scrooge" Jack. I don't spend a cent more than I have to. I'm not taking an R&R because it costs too much. So up to now, I have $600 in the Soldier's deposit and Finance owes me about $400 but the jerks say they need me on the line, so I can't get in, to get it fixed. By the next letter I write I will have made Spec-4 which will get me another $60 in the bank in a month. And if I do extend, I will be a Sergeant and putting two hundred and 75 in the bank a month. Did they ever fix my bonds?

Everybody's ribbing me calling me Sergeant York and Audie Murphy because of my medals. They said they thought I was going to be a dud because I was a journalist and everything.

Did you get my Purple Heart in the mail? How's the colored TV set? Beautiful I bet. You know that Bill guy I said was from Cincinnati and took music and piano at UC and was hit at Loc Ninh. Well he lost his arm. It's a shame because he really could play very well.

Also, that Sergeant who was over here 42 months. Well he got killed by an RPG round. He had a wife and 4 kids.

Things have quieted down since Loc Ninh. We've been out here since the beginning of December and will be here until January 15. Our battalion killed about 100 gooks since we've been out here. The place where we're at is called Casson 6.

I got a Christmas card from Bob G. I haven't heard from Bill since I've been here.

Some nut was here yesterday asking for guys to join the MACVI Recon team. All it is, is where they send you in two-man teams and you go over the DMZ to scout and mark targets for the jets. You may even go to Hanoi. The only thing is that your chances are almost nil of returning. I told him to go jump in the lake. Only one man took it and that guy is a little nutty.

By the way, how's Jerri doing at UC? Did she do well on her tests? Does she still have her scholarship? If she or you need any money take it out of my account. It might be a while before I use it.

About school. I still definitely plan to go back to Villa Madonna and take political science. I know now what an education means and how much it helps. But I don't regret the time in the Army because it makes a man out of you. And teaches you discipline and patience, two very important virtues. It also teaches you appreciation for the things you had before you came in.

About that Bob Hope show, his guests were Phil Crosby, Barbara McNair, Raquel Welch, and Miss World, and some Broadway singer and Carl Wilson. Hope really put down Johnson on the entire show.

I'm almost positive that Johnson will be defeated by either Nixon or Romney. I hope Nixon gets elected. I don't know about that Romney. The only way Johnson will be elected is to have Bob Kennedy for his vice-presidential running mate, which will never happen.

The VC won't sign any treaty over here. Why should they. They can beat us. Simply by waiting us out. The VC will simply just retreat to the North and just wait us out. We can't afford to keep everything combat ready. Things will quiet down. We can't financially keep all these troops and equipment in combat readiness. So, we'd begin a gradual pull back. Then the VC would come back and start at his old tricks.

Another thing he could do is to stop fighting here and move over to another country like Thailand or Laos and start all over again. This Southeast Asia is a perpetual powder keg. They've been fighting over here since time began. And if Johnson and his boys could see that these people just simply don't care who rules them. All they know is that the American dollar can buy them pretty much all things. Other than that, they could care who rules them.

If we keep fighting this war the way we have been fighting it, I believe we will win the battles but lose the war. I believe the US should declare war on North Vietnam and bomb the North with B-52 bombers. Then blacktop it. And if the Chinese and Russia don't like it, we'll do the same to them too. Now is the time to call their bluff. Not until they are strong enough to defeat us and I believe if we did this, we'd have the same results Kennedy had when he called the bluff of Russia in the Cuban and Berlin Crises.

If we'd only do this America wouldn't look like a fool to the rest of the world, as she does today, and I bet the people of the US would be surprised to see how the war would end so quickly. Sure, it's a big chance but it's a chance we must take. If we don't take that chance, we'll be over here twenty years from now and have been fighting for twenty years but wouldn't have accomplished anything but making a few men millionaires.

What I'm afraid of is that one of these doves (Romney) will get in office and end the war dishonorably. We have to win this war and fight it to the end. Simply to prove to the Communists that America won't get tired of fighting this war, like a child with a new toy, and once we commit ourselves to something, we won't pull out when we get tired. America has been over here for close to 6 years and we could end this war in three days if we wanted to (that's not even using atomic bombs). Westmoreland is even quoted as saying that. I just hope whoever gets in realizes this fact and ends this war as soon as possible. I went a little overboard.

How's the kids doing? Fine, I hope. I hope they had a fine Christmas and that Santa was good to them. I got Jeff's letter with Jim's picture. Why don't you send me a few pictures of everyone if you don't mind? Tell Judy to be good. Are all the cars acting up lately with the cold weather? If they have to get fixed, use my money. Tell Dad I said hello and to take it easy. It's getting dark now, so I better be going. I'll write again soon.

Love,

Jack

A TOUCH OF HOME: ENTERTAINMENT

THE ENTERTAINMENT OF MILITARY FORCES is not-an altogether recent event, except perhaps in our era. Entire Roman legions were entertained by mimes whose art had derived from Greek classical theatre.

Perhaps one reason why live entertainment is so in demand in Vietnam is the nature of the war. Since there is no such thing as a "front," neither is there any "rear" in the conventional military sense. The rear has commonly included club shows and commercial entertainment. Today, in such an atmosphere, television sets and recreational opportunities might also flourish. But to many, if not most units in Vietnam, the rear is not a question of distance it simply doesn't exist. Live entertainment is usually the only entertainment. The further and more protracted troop removal is from an atmosphere of security, the more intense becomes the desire for live entertainment—and the greater the need for a touch of home.

The BIG RED ONE had only been in Vietnam a few months before its first live entertainment arrived. It came in grand style: Bob Hope, Martha Raye, Ann-Margret and Edgar Bergan all brought shows to Di An, Phu Loi, and Phuoc Yinh in late 1965 and early 1966.

The entertainment provided to 1st Division troops has since been widely varied, although some established forms have scarcely played here at all. Vocalists, combos, and a blend of the two have appeared with frequency. Allied nations, such as Korea and Australia, have lent us a variety of shows with universal success. "Entertainment" has ranged all the way from a lavish spectacle to a single unaccompanied individual. Any number of musical groups have appeared, with names as far out as their "combo" music—the "Holy Buckets," the "Sinister Soul Set," and "Monday's Children" among them.

Another successful variety of entertainment has been provided by vocalists: especially Nancy Sinatra at Lai Khe in February, and Connie Francis at Di An in December 1967. The men wanted the songs which had been best-selling records at home, and they weren't disappointed when "These Boots Were Made for Walking," and "Where the Boys Are," were sung by their originators.

In terms of time spent in Vietnam and total troops entertained, Martha Raye has no equal. She has toured the country repeatedly, extended for a longer stay, and then after a period in the States—such as for her Broadway appearance in "Hello Dolly"—returned. No one has become better known or more loved by the troops.

Girls have been an indispensable ingredient in the success of the most lavish and looked-forward-to productions in Vietnam, the Christmas shows of Honorary 1st Division Member Bob Hope, dean of all troop entertainers in our era. The first Bob Hope show to play to a BIG RED ONE audience since War II took place at Di An in 1965. He returned to Di An in 1966, and at Lai Khe in 1967 he played to an audience of 8,000.[14]

USO PERFORMANCES

TET OFFENSIVE
JANUARY 30-FEBRUARY 24, 1968

DURING THE WANING DAYS of January, the enemy seemed to be avoiding contact with elements of the BIG RED ONE. However, because of massive supply movements by the VC, many high echelon commanders were fearful of some kind of all-out enemy offensive.

At 0300 hours on 31 January 1968, the day that marked the beginning of the Lunar New Year for Orientals, the enemy attacked 35 major population centers and virtually all major allied basecamps throughout the Republic of Vietnam.

Saigon in the south and the ancient city of Hue in the north were the focal points of the attack. In Saigon the VC unleashed a suicide attack on the US Embassy and held the building for several hours before being routed by paratroopers and military police. Street fighting in both Saigon and Hue continued throughout the first five days of February.

The First Infantry Division's headquarters at Lai Khe came under a heavy rocket, mortar and recoilless rifle attack that lasted nearly an hour. When this attack ceased, the enemy struck at the Army of the Republic of Vietnam (ARVN) outpost at Hen Cat, one mile south of Lai Khe. The ARVN'S call for assistance was responded to immediately with helicopter gunships, artillery and cavalry support from the Big Red One. Airstrikes from Bien Hoa Air Base were also called in on the attackers. Contact was broken at dawn and a sweep of the area turned up 48 enemy bodies.

A few hours later the Division was called on to help secure the huge Tan Son Nhut Air base complex, home of the headquarters of the Military Assistance Command, Vietnam (MACV). The 1st Battalion, 18th Infantry and A Troop, 1st Squadron, 4th Cavalry, were immediately moved to the base, where they killed 16 enemy in their first contact.

In several scattered contacts during the first day of the TET OFFENSIVE, Division elements accounted for more than 80 enemy killed. The first day of February was marked by scattered heavy contacts throughout the division area of operation, including a savage battle around the village of An My, 20 miles north of Saigon.

AN MY

AT 0920 HOURS ON 1 FEBRUARY 1968, Company C, 1st Battalion, 28th Infantry, and a platoon of B Troop, 1st Squadron, 4th Cavalry, departed the Phu Loi basecamp enroute to a reconnaissance-in-force mission through the village of An My, less than a mile from the north gate.

Friendly casualties during the first day of the BATTLE OF AN MY were 5 killed and 43 wounded. Enemy losses were 197 killed by body count and 120 detained. Sixty-five of the total killed were reported by aerial observers and the large number of detainees came from the screening of individuals leaving the village earlier in the day.

The 3rd Platoon and the ARP swept the area, finding 30 enemy bodies. A Company losses were 9 killed and 2 wounded.

The sweep of An My was completed at approximately 1900 hours. Interrogation of detainees revealed the enemy force to be elements of the 273d VC Regiment. Total VC losses during the two-day BATTLE OF AN MY were 372 killed. US losses were 18 killed and 49 wounded.

XOM MOI 1

ON 2 FEBRUARY 1968 A Troop, 1st Squadron, 4th Cavalry became OPCON in Xom Moi, north of Tan Son Nhut Air Base. The heaviest volume of fire was coming from the western end of the village. VC losses to A Troop were 46 killed. US losses were only 14 wounded.

BIG RED ONE units at Tan Son Nhut killed six enemy and found 79 bodies killed earlier. A total of 143 enemy dead were accounted for by Division units during the day. During the next two days, 4 and 5 February, the action became more and more scattered and sporadic as the VC offensive lost momentum.

Although the enemy gained the offensive for a short period of time, TET can be classified as a total failure. The sneak offensive, planned, according to intelligence sources, as far back as September 1967, cost the enemy 21,330 killed from 1800 hours on 29 January through 2400 hours 5 February. More than 60,000 communists participated in the offensive. Allied losses during the week were 1,729, including 546 Americans.[15]

Vietnam Tet Offensive 1968

March 1968

Dear Mom and Dad,

Well I'm finally getting a letter off today. I know it's been so long and I'm sorry.

Let's see, at Christmas I was on Highway 13 on Christmas day as you know. Then we proceeded to Lai Khe, the first week in January. After a short stay we went to Ben Cat and stayed there a week. Then the next week we went to Phu Loi for a short stay. Then we went back to Lai Khe for two days and that's when our trouble began. February first and second is when the Vietnamese celebrate the Lunar New Year and is when the VC staged the biggest offensive since the beginning of the war.

I tell you it was bad. They don't tell you how bad it really was back in the world.

The VC attacked every major base and city in South Vietnam. And when I mean attacked, they literally over ran it.

At Lai Khe we were getting artillery fire from our own artillery pieces the VC captured. Those rockets and mortars and artillery were really cleaning up at Lai Khe. So then on February 2ⁿᵈ they moved us to Saigon at Tan Son Nhut to guard MACVI Headquarters (the place where Westmoreland lives). We were the only unit of the 1ˢᵗ Infantry Division to be allowed to come into Saigon. They attacked us once but there were no casualties. It's hard to believe the damage that's been done to the cities and villages.

We go into a village with tanks and personnel carriers and if there's any VC sniper or fire, we simply level the place, civilians and all.

We had quite a firefight the other day at this cloth factory. We lost two men. One who was here as long as I have been, the other was here two weeks. Our medic was hit, a friend of mine had his eyes knocked out by fragmentation. Another got shot in the foot. Another got it in the chest.

We killed about 50 of them though.

The factory was huge, and it was a complete loss. The people don't know where to go. Hundreds of families are without homes to go to cause the VC has them or we have destroyed them.

It's just one big mess. I heard yesterday that they rocketed the airstrip again and hit a waiting station for GI's who were going home. One was killed and 20 were wounded. We left Tan Son Nhut a week ago and now at Thu Duc about two miles out of Bien Hoa.

We had to clean out the VC from the city. We've done that, so now we eagle flight (that's chopper out in the morning and come back at night) to other villages and clean them out.

I hate to talk about this mess, it's senseless to.

The other day we had to go out and help the 1st of the 28th Infantry and did they get hit.

They made a gross mistake though. When they made the first initial contact they pulled back (like they're supposed to) and called in air strikes, gunships and artillery. But the only thing, they did this, but they left 15 men there and they were killed by our own jets and artillery. We had to go in and get the bodies. It was a shame. No use in talking about it though.

Some good news though. Well I made Spec 4 last month so you can drop PFC. The platoon Sergeant put me in for Sergeant because I am a point man and team leader for our squad. I also go on R&R this month to Australia. Also, I got my Silver Star from Westmoreland while we were at MACVI Headquarters. He said the 1st 18th was the best Army combat unit in Vietnam. They said they'd send it home so you should be getting it shortly. I don't know when I'll get my Bronze Star, probably in May they said. Well by the time you receive this letter, I'll be starting the ninth month. It doesn't seem that long though.

I think I'll extend in May when we go back to Di An to go home. I saw a buddy of mine who said he saw my orders and said I got Korea. If this is true, I'll stay here another year if I have to. I can handle things here, but I know it would be too cold for me there. I come home in May for a 30 day leave so expect me home in May.

Well I've talked too much already and it's time for bed. Take it easy and don't worry.

Love,

Jack

P.S. Tell everyone hello. I've been getting all your packages. The paper stopped. I get your gum and Kool Aid and I appreciate it. Tell John and Grandmother thanks for the Valentine Card.

Loc Ninh Base

CHAPTER SEVEN

APRIL 1968-SEPTEMBER 1968

A BRONZE STAR AND MAYBE GOING HOME

Most of the ink Jack used in the letters in this chapter focused on how much time he had remaining in Vietnam. Typical tours were a year long. Jack's 3-year enlistment started on December 30, 1966. His Vietnam tour began on June 30, 1967 so he was planning on leaving the country on June 30, 1968 then being stationed at Ft. Hood, Texas.

Jack's unit was stationed at the Army's Lai Khe installation in April and their mission was to find Viet Cong rocket sites used to bomb the base. He learned he got a promotion to Sergeant E-5 and was excited his Vietnam tour was ending. Jack planned to be home possibly by the end of June and no one in the family remembered the time frames he visited but he must have gone home during early summer 1968.

On May 4, Jack's company engaged the enemy in battle northeast of Di An and he killed several Viet Cong soldiers then chased the retreating enemy and killed several more, earning him a Bronze Star with V for Valor.

He indicated he was tired, and that unit morale was low. Jack was losing many friends he served with. Vietnamese children being used to set booby traps troubled him. The Bobby Kennedy and Martin Luther King assassinations disappointed him. He got ill and lost weight, but he was taken off risky point duty and became a squad leader, which meant no night Listening, no day Observation posts and another potential promotion.

He enjoyed R&R in Australia in April where he shopped and danced then had a 3-day pass at Vung Tau, Vietnam, known for some of the best beaches on the South China Sea. Our mother was surprised about Jack's, apparently new, dancing affinity, but I like to envision him moving around the floors to great music with dates and new friends, forgetting horrific war images, at least for a few hours. Music was common in our house growing up. Jack loved the Motown sound and he had several albums and 45s from that label. I hope the Aussie jukeboxes had his favorites.

In early June 1968, Jack seemed convinced he had 2 ambushes and 2 patrols left in the field. At the time he didn't admit there were more war battles in his future but he considered extending his tour at various times, so before leaving for home he decided to return to his unit and comrades after his first year in Vietnam.

April 6, 1968

Dear Mom and Dad,

Well I'm finally writing. I know it's been a long time, but I just don't know what to write.

At the max I've got 83 days to go. The time sure has been flying. That means I've got 73 field days but now if we go home by boat, we will leave May 31st and that means 43 more days. If things go right, I'll be Sergeant at the end of this month. Also, I'm taking my 7 day leave for Australia the 20th of the month in which I'll have 20 days out in the field. 23 field days.

I didn't get my Bronze Star yet, but I'll probably get that before we go home.

We are working out of Lai Khe. Our job is just to find the rocket sites the VC are using to bomb Lai Khe. So far, we are unsuccessful.

Isn't that terrible about Martin Luther King.

The next place I'm putting in for is the Berlin Brigade in Germany. I hope just to ETS (get out of the Army) from there. They say they treat you very nice if you're a veteran and if you're E-5.

President Johnson is sure screwing things up. I'd say it will be Nixon or McCarthy. I hope Nixon wins.

Well I've got one big change to tell you. I've been in the 1st 18th Reconnaissance team since Christmas. We do mostly night work, night patrols, sniper duty, and checking out areas. We work mostly in 5-man teams. There's only 20 of us and they treat us like kings.

Love,

Jack

MAY 1968 BATTLES

OPERATION TOAN THANG

TAN HIEP

ON THE MORNING of 4 May 1968, Company D, 1st Battalion, 18th Infantry departed the Di An base camp to conduct a reconnaissance-in-force mission near the village of Tan Hiep, two miles to the north.

Local intelligence reports indicated that the villagers of Tan Hiep were being forced to store ammunition for the enemy. As the Swamp Rats approached the village, it became apparent that the inhabitants had deserted since no activity could be seen.

While searching the surrounding area—a 300 by 400-yard clearing in the woods crossed by irrigation ditches—the 1st Platoon contacted an unknown size enemy force along the wood line on the northern side of the clearing. Thus, the BATTLE OF TAN HIEP began.

The BATTLE OF TAN HIEP cost the enemy 245 killed. BIG RED ONE troops captured a large assortment of enemy materiel, including 40 individual and 8 crew-served weapons. US casualties were 6 killed and 20 wounded.

Captain Shaw described the Viet Cong soldiers as "well-equipped and well-fed." "Their weapons were in mint condition" he added, "and many of them carried clean, starched civilian clothes wrapped in plastic bags."

On the morning immediately following the BATTLE OF TAN HIEP the communists officially launched their second offensive (later to be called the 5 MAY OFFENSIVE) by raining mortars and rockets on the capital city of Saigon.

XOM MOI II

At 1330 hours on 5 May, after four days of continuous RIF operations from the Di An base camp, Troop B sighted an enemy soldier just to the west of the village of Xom Moi. While engaging him, two more the enemy jumped from their hiding places in the ground and tried to flee. All three were brought down and the BATTLE OF XOM MOI II began.

A psychological operations (PSYOPS) team flew over the area. "Soldiers of the North Vietnamese and VC force," came the announcement, "you are going to be attacked relentlessly from the air and from the ground. We will hold our fire for five minutes. If you desire to surrender, come out in the open field and raise your hands."

No one came out.

Captain Scates recalled that after the PSYOPS ship flew away, the cavalry again moved into position. "We began receiving light fire from VC on our flanks. Then we found those 50-calibers which had been there the day before. The NVA hadn't moved them at all. I spread my vehicles out around one of the larger ravines and the infantry swept down into the eroded gully. The LOHs (light observation helicopters) saw a lot of VC running around and took them with minigun fire."

During the next several days, sporadic action continued but the battle was over. The action inflicted heavy losses on the enemy: 440 killed and many wounded. Captured were machineguns, rice, AK47 ammunition, 60mm mortars, 12.7mm ammunition, 30 pounds of medicine, and numerous other weapons and equipment. US losses were 3 killed and 21 wounded.[16]

JACK'S JUNE R&R DESTINATION: VUNG TAU, VIETNAM

May 16, 1968

Dear Mom and Dad,

Well only 44 days at the max. Now I have 38 field days left. I'll be going to the rear for a 3-day pass at Vung Tau in June. It will be good to get home again. I've got my orders and it's Fort Hood, Texas. I think I'm getting 45-day leave, so I'll have pretty much enough time.

Also, some more good news. At the end of May I'll be a Sergeant E-5, so I'll be happy.

Things are a little down right now. The monsoon is here again. We were hit pretty hard. A lot of my good buddies got it the other day in my old company. Maybe it was luck or something, but I left for Recon three days before Delta Company was hit. My old platoon was on point. I would have been walking point. The guy who took my place walking point got blown apart. Out of the 22 men who went out, only 5 made it back without a scratch. So maybe it was lucky I came to Recon.

After I spend a few months in the states I'm going to put in for the Berlin Brigade in Germany. It's good duty and with my job being an intelligence-operation reconnaissance Sergeant it won't be too bad. They like guys who've been decorated a few times.

By the way, I'll be sending my two Bronze Stars with V and my Army commendation home. I think I'm going to get an Air Medal too and my two Vietnamese campaign ribbons to send home.

Man did I have a good time down in Australia. The people were out of this world. They treated us great and Sydney is the cleanest, friendliest city in the world. They don't have fights, riots or any other disturbances. The average income of an Australian is between $3-4000 a year. A person with a degree from the states could come down and make 10 thousand dollars a year salary without too much sweat. They love American people and at night it doesn't matter who you are, every man you see has a sport coat or a suit on and every woman is dressed up.

I honestly wouldn't mind going down there and live after a few years. You can get a new American car (with the steering wheel switched to the other side) for about 2 grand. Their dollar is worth more than ours. Our dollar is 89 cents to their dollar. I bought some nice clothes for a nice price. One tweed sport coat and one good-looking suit. Really nice things.

I turned in my M-14 rifle and now I'm carrying an M-16. It's a lot lighter but a little less dependable.

I was sitting here thinking and it's surprising how few of us are left who originally came over here. A lot of guys were killed, and others were wounded. The way it looks, they're just trying to get the rest of us. By sending us out on ambushes every night, long patrols.

Charlie has his stuff together and it's getting worse. Little kids are being trained to set out booby traps when they come begging for food. You really must watch out. Like I said before, the times you must watch out for is your first 3 months and your last two. You can just see guys trying to get out of the field for anything, so they won't have to go out.

We are just waiting around for Saigon to break out again. I hope it doesn't.

I've made a lot of friends over here and being on the line makes us about as close as brothers. Everybody watches out for everybody else. You see new faces come in (always so eager to get out in the action).

I'm getting tired. We had one guy who I owe my life to. Mac (an A&P Supermarket produce manager) was walking second to me on point. Suddenly, he yells "Look out Jack!" and a damn gook sticks his weapon out and smacks me on the shoulder with it. I fell down and as I fell, he fired about 5 rounds and then Mac wounded him, and I finished him off.

The people here think I'm a little crazy cause I hate these people so much. The only thing I hate more than a gook is crap in a latrine and if I got a chance to get a few of them, I will do it. I didn't think I'd ever feel about anything or anyone like this, but I hate them all.

Well I figure on digging about one more hole and that will be the last hole I ever dig.

Is Bill F. still in the hospital? I hope he is getting along well.

There goes a jerk now running around with a camera taking pictures. I wish to hell if he was so darn interested in us, he wouldn't just come up, stick the damn thing in our face and snap the shutter.

How's Bill M. doing? Tell him to go into the Air Force. He comes into the Army; he'll regret it every day he is over here.

Well it's starting to rain now, and I have to get ready for ambush, so I better get going. Pretty soon it will be over, and I'll be home, so take care and don't worry. Tell Dad to take it easy and not to worry. How's Jerri doing now with her art? Tell Jeff, Jim and Judy I said hello and to be good. Well that's about it. Don't worry!

Love,

Jack

P.S. Excuse the condition of the letter because it got wet.

May 28, 1968

Dear Mom and Dad,

Well things are going pretty well now. Time is going fast. Today I have thirty-two days at the max in country and 27 days left in the field at the max. That's not too bad. Those jerks at the rear still haven't sent out the E-5 orders yet. They are just too lazy to bother to make them out or what, I just don't know.

Rain is in its full swing now. They have us just outside of the Saigon area guarding some bridge where 5 VC battalions are supposed to hit. Don't worry because in every case we have caught them before they've hit the bridge.

It's filthy here, we've nicknamed the place "fly alley". It is just an alley with a dump on the other side.

I decided to go to Ft. Hood for a month or two then go to Berlin Brigade for a year and that will be it. I'll take a proficiency pay test to get $30 more, then overseas pay and after I've been in the Army two years, I'll get a $160 raise.

I think I'm going to put in for a 3 month drop so I can start school in September. I think I can get it. I've got 18 months in the Army at the end of June. Just another 18 to go. You figure another 2 months goes to leave. That leaves 16 months. I'm guaranteed 12 months in Germany and if I could get a 3 month drop, well just another year.

It's starting to rain now so I better be going now so don't worry. Tell everyone I said hello.

Love,

Jack

TOAN THANG PHASE II: JUNE-AUGUST 1968

PHASE I OF OPERATION TOAN THANG officially ended 31 May after heavy losses had been inflicted on NVA and VC forces. Phase I was immediately followed on 1 Tune by Phase II of the operation which, as in the previous phase, involved all allied troops in the III Corps Tactical Zone. Night ambushes, reconnaissance-in-force missions (RIFs), numerous engagements and the locating of enemy supply caches highlighted Phase II of Operation TOAN THANG during the months of June, July and early August.

Company C, 2nd Battalion, 18th Infantry captured 22 107mm rockets five miles east of Saigon in early June. On 4 July Company A, 2nd Battalion, 28th Infantry located a giant stockpile of enemy weapons, including 55 rockets and more than 1,100 RPG rounds, just west of the BIG RED ONE'S Lai Khe headquarters. One day prior to this find, Company C, 2nd Battalion, 18th Infantry captured 44 107mm rockets and 18 122mm rockets in a heavily vegetated area six miles east of Saigon.

Enemy activity began to pick up again during the latter part of August with especially heavy movement noted in the Loc Ninh area, 70 miles north of Saigon. BIG RED ONE elements increased RIF (reconnaissance-in-force) missions as they became involved in some of the hardest fighting since the 5 MAY OFFENSIVE.[17]

June 6, 1968

Dear Mom and Dad,

Well today is the 6th so that puts us with 14 days left in the field and twenty-two days left in country and by June 30th, I should be home. Well 3 guys who came over on the boat with me got it the other day. They were riding on a truck and hit a mine. They blew up right in front of my position. They didn't know what hit them. It's too bad about Kennedy. He had all those kids.

My allocation for E-5 didn't come down yet. They are screwing me on that. They want me to extend but I don't know. I will be home for July if I do extend or not. I've been sick and lost a few pounds since last week. I'm going to have to get up and live again when I get home. This place works on your mind after a while, if you let it. You ought to see the guys who are mentally unstable. I wouldn't even walk down the street with them at home, let alone go out on ambush with them.

I've gotten off point (point man scout) and taken over a squad (11 men). With a squad I wouldn't have to do much if I did extend. Just take them out on squad size ambushes and patrols. No LP's or OP's (listening posts at night or observation posts during the day) and I'd make E-6 out of it probably.

Morale is pretty low lately. The men they are sending from the states aren't worth a darn. If you'd talk to them, you wouldn't think they cared if they lived or died. They don't care about something good or bad if they have to work some to get it. All of them just curse and moan if you tell them to do something. The US is really scraping the bottom of the barrel for the jerks they're sending over here. It's too bad. A lot of good men are getting it because of these duds fresh from the states. I got your's and Jerri's letters. That's good about the hospital job. I'm going to have to meet Jerri's boyfriend.

He sounds pretty interesting. That was great about the 4-Tops concert. That's my favorite group. Tell Jerri to clue me in on any discotheques in the city cause Jack's a dancing fool now. I went down to Australia and all I did was dance down there. I'm sending my civilian clothes home that I used for R&R.

From what I understand, Ft. Hood is just a dust bowl but what the guys like is that it's real close to Mexico. If I did extend, I'd have 11 months at the max in the Army and they couldn't send me anywhere but back to the states. If I play my cards right, I could have a 3 month early out to start school in September of 1969 instead of December.

How are Bill M. and Bill F. doing? Fine, I hope. It would be a shame to miss Bill M. in July. Tell Dad, Jeff and Jim that we'll catch a ball game when I get home. You and Dad are going out on a night on the town when I get home. I don't know exactly how or where yet. Take care.

Love,

Jack

BIG RED ONE STRATEGY is mapped out by (from left) Lieutenant Colonel William G. Benedict, division G-2; Lieutenant Colonel Richard E. Cavazos, 1st Battalion, 18th Infantry, commander; Brigadier General William S. Coleman, assistant division commander; and Major James M. Tucker, battalion S-3.

Commanders Planning Strategy

June 10, 1968

Dear Mom and Dad,

Well today I have 19 days at the max left in country. That puts us 10 days left in the field. I have 2 patrols and 2 ambushes left. I'd just thought I'd write to keep you clued on the progress.

It's raining constantly now. It's hard to keep anything dry. Westmoreland will be leaving in July, so I don't know what's going to happen now.

That's a shame about Kennedy. His politics were a little radical, but he had a big family. I look for the father (Joe) to kick off pretty soon. I'll have to look up Butch when I get home. Graduating from high school already.

Do you think Jerri will get her scholarship renewed?

From the 24th on you don't have to write because I'll be in transit stage and I won't get them. I'll be cleared out of company and battalion and be at Long Binh from the 25th on and could leave the country any time after the 25th. I'll try to call when I get to the states if I can.

Well it's starting to rain so I better be going. So, take care and don't worry. Tell everyone I said hello.

Love,

Jack

JUNE 6-SEPTEMBER 13, 1968
BATTLES

XOM BUNG JUNE 6, 1968

While conducting a search four miles southeast of Lai Khe, Company A, 2nd/18th Infantry, 1st Infantry Division entered the base camp of the VC Phu Loi Bn and made heavy contact. The 2nd Mechanized Infantry reinforced along with air and artillery. The battle raged throughout the day. A sweep that evening revealed 58 VC dead but FACs estimated there were 15 more in areas the Inf could not reach. The 2nd/18th was extracted back to FSB Normandy I. Artillery was applied all night and the next day the 2nd/18th air-assaulted the area again. Their sweep turned up an additional 27 VC KIAs for a total of 100.

LOC III NINH

On the night of 22 August, the village of Loc Ninh was burned by the NVA. In reaction to this, and because large numbers of the enemy were known to be in the vicinity, the 1st Battalion, 2nd Infantry, commanded by Lieutenant Colonel Thomas E. Fitzpatrick, conducted a reconnaissance-in-force mission five miles east of the village.

The fighting continued until late morning. After the smoke cleared, the friendly elements found 29 enemy bodies and captured a 60mm mortar, six rocket launchers, 10 AK rifles and numerous hand grenades and B-40 rockets. The Black Scarves moved back up the hill and Company D secured a landing zone (LZ) while equipment and casualties were flown out.

"There were dead NVA everywhere," recalled Lieutenant Jones. "We found a complex consisting of about 20 bunkers on top of the hill. The strange thing about the whole fight was that the enemy had excellent fields of fire in the open terrain, but we received very little AK rifle fire. Nearly all was from 82mm mortars. It was idiotic! It seemed as if they were trying to get close enough to throw RPG rounds at us." The week-long battle cost the enemy 200 dead, plus many weapons, supplies and equipment. Allied losses were five killed and 75 wounded.

LOC IV NINH

On 11 September, the 1st Battalion, 2nd Infantry, consisting of Companies C and D, was diverted to the rubber tree area east of Loc Ninh to establish a blocking position. On 12 September the two companies were to conduct reconnaissance missions further eastward but again heavy enemy resistance was encountered.

Company C dug in for the night about 800 yards from Hill 222. There was movement throughout the night, but there was no evidence of the enemy the following morning (the 13th). In sweeping the battlefield one dead NVA soldier with documents and two AK weapons were found.

During the early afternoon of 13 September, the command helicopter carrying Major General Keith L. Ware, commander of the BIG RED ONE, Command Sergeant Major Joseph A. Venable, and six others, crashed and burned due to hostile fire south and east of Loc Ninh. There were no survivors in the crash. The Assistant Division Commander, Major General Orwin C. Talbott, immediately assumed command of the 1st Infantry Division.

After two days of light action following the link-up at Hill 222, all units returned to their base camps and the fourth BATTLE OF LOC NINH was over.

The five-day engagement resulted in 216 enemy killed, and numerous weapons and equipment, including six machine-guns and 13 AK-47s, were taken by allied elements. US casualties were 33 killed.[18]

THE BATTLE OF LOC NINH

" NO MISSION TOO DIFFICULT, NO SACRIFICE TOO GREAT, DUTY FIRST"

THE AMERICAN TRAVELER

Vol. 28, No. 44   1st Infantry Division   Republic of Vietnam   November 11, 1967

Nearly 1000 Enemy Killed In Fighting At Loc Ninh

By PFC John Reno

(Div IO) — American and Vietnamese forces in and around Loc Ninh killed 865 Viet Cong in heavy fighting which erupted Oct 29 and continued through Nov 2.

The first engagement began at 7 a.m. on Oct 29, with elements of the 273d VC Regiment attacking the village of Loc Ninh some 70 miles north of Saigon where CIDG and ARVN forces were lodged, overrunning portions of the perimeter and entering the village itself. The families there when the village was retaken by allied forces, were later evacuated to An Loc and are under the care of the BIG RED ONE which is providing food and clothing for them.

Next Morning

The next morning, men from the 1st Infantry Division teamed up with the US Special Forces and Vietnamese forces to retake the village from the VC. This proved to be difficult as the communists put up stubborn resistance in street-type fighting and used the perimeter bunkers they had taken the night before. When the action finally broke off with the enemy fleeing, the total killed inside the perimeter was 92 Viet Cong.

The enemy ran from the village but their escape had been foreseen by the 1st Bn, 2d Div CG, MG John H. Hay, who had set up an infantry battalion, the 1st Bn, 18th Inf, as a blocking force.

Enemy Fled

As the enemy fled through the heavy jungle, they ran into the blocking force, which killed another 40 enemy.

The day after the first battle Loc Ninh was filled with activity as the « Swamp Rats » of the 1st Bn, 18th Inf, ran across a VC company south of their night defensive posi-

tion (NDP) two miles west of the village.

A and D companies of the « Swamp Rats » were moving toward their NDP when they surprised the enemy. During the battle which ensued, the Viet Cong retreated to higher ground in a rubber plantation.

« Rebels » reported 20 VC killed (body count) and an estimated 80 Viet Cong killed in the fighting, bringing the enemy death toll to 228 for the first two days of fighting.

October 31, the third day of the action, started as the 2d Bn, 28th Inf « Black Lions »

began firing harassment and interdiction mortar fire, only to have it returned an hour later.

Helicopter light fire teams, artillery and air strikes were again called in as the enemy fire decreased from heavy to (See Enemy Losses, Page 8)

Members of the 2d Battalion, 28th Infantry move into the embattled village with recoilless rifles. The 90 mm recoilless rifle proved very effective after they who had occupied bunkers after overrunning a portion of the perimeter.
Photo by SP4 George Pawlaczyk

Recoilless Rifles Rout Enemy From Bunkers

By SP4 M. F. Robinson

(Div IO) — The men of the Division's 2d Battalion, 28th Infantry, wasted no time when their recoilless rifle team was called into the action during the recent battle at Loc Ninh.

Finding the Viet Cong entrenched in heavily-fortified bunkers in the rubber tree

about five miles south of the Cambodian border.

Air and artillery strikes were called and « Rebel » gunships from A Co, 1st Aviation Bn, assisted in the fight. After contact was broken in the late afternoon, the

covered town, SP4 Clarence Reese, Oakland, Calif., along with SP4 Lawrence Hartman of Salisbury, Mo., were brought from Quan Loi to aid the other companies engaged in the battle.

Brandishing 90 mm recoilless rifles, the two men rushed (See Recoilless, Page 8)

The following message was forwarded from General W.C. Westmoreland, Commander U.S. Forces, Vietnam :

The response of your Forces, especially elements of the 1st Infantry Division, to the enemy attack on Loc Ninh on 29 October was an outstanding example of aggressive, timely and effective exploitation of a tactical opportunity presented by the enemy. I extend to you and to the officers and men of the 1st Infantry Division my personal congratulations.

I would like to add my personal congratulations to every man in the Big Red One who participated in the operations against the 9th Viet Cong Division. It was a truly outstanding accomplishment and a major setback for the enemy. Let me add my sincere congratulations and appreciation for a job well done.

John H. Hay
Major General, USA
Commanding

Air, Artillery Pound VC

By SP4 George Pawlaczyk

During the night attack on November 2, the most savage of a series of attacks on Loc Ninh and the surrending area, jet fighters which flew over 100 sorties during this single battle, dodged 50 caliber machinegun tracers as they pounded an enemy regiment attacking the 1st Bn, 18th Inf. It was at this battalion's location that BIG RED ONE infantrymen came up against enemy soldiers armed with flamethrowers.

Flamethrower

One flamethrower-armed VC got within 20 yards of the American perimeter. « He got close enough to use his flame but he didn't know we were there, » said machinegunner SP4 Glenn Gillian, Loudonderry, Ohio. « We shot him and he exploded.»

Nearby, at the Special Forces compound, enemy « suicide » assaults met with disasterous losses as Division artillery fired point blank down the airstrip at Loc Ninh.

Hundreds

As hundreds of enemy attempted to cross the airstrip to overrun the Special Forces outpost, 105 mm fragmentary rounds fired from the south end of the runway by the 6th Bn, 15th Arty, killed scores of VC in midstride.

« We couldn't see anything because of the smoke,» said artilleryman PFC Donald Broussard of A Btry. « We received the request for bursts right down the runway from the Special Forces camp, » explained Broussard w h o is (See Air and Arty, Page 8)

Ramrods Find Factory

(3d Bde IO) — A maze of boobytraps led to the discovery of a VC supply and munitions factory recently as the Division's 2d Battalion (Mech), 28 Infantry swept the jungles ten miles north of Lai Khe.

After the boobytraps were disarmed or blown in place, the (See Factory, Page 8)

CHAPTER EIGHT

SEPTEMBER-DECEMBER 1968

A SECOND CHRISTMAS IN VIETNAM

Jack extended his tour in June 1968 and returned to Vietnam as a Sergeant. He indicated it would likely be his final extension although Jack mused he might stay longer so it would be warm when he returned home.

He believed he would be stationed at Fort Jackson, SC after leaving Vietnam and repeated his desire to return to college and study Political Science.

His attitude toward the war and the Army deteriorated although he indicated he would consider working in Vietnam as a civilian. He had a fight with his Sergeant Major and blamed superior officer incompetence for comrades getting killed. Jack criticized US politicians and the peace process although our mother remembers him vigorously endorsing Richard Nixon for president since Jack believed Nixon would end the war. Jack claimed he will be a war dissenter after he gets back home, which surprised me since our father said Jack believed helping South Vietnam defeat the Northern Viet Cong would stop the spread of Communism in southeast Asia.

Jack earned another Bronze Star on October 21, 1968, when, as a squad leader, he led his men to successfully engage Viet Cong soldiers, allowing another squad to overrun the enemy position. He earned the Soldier's Medal on November 25, 1968 for pulling injured crew from a crashed, burning helicopter a second time, while munitions on board exploded and stayed at the scene to help assist with medical attention to the wounded.

Jack and his squad finished 1968 on patrols and ambushes even though they had trouble getting enough water for drinking and hygiene. They were all courageous heroes committed to service and to each other. Jack's December letter indicated his last day in the field would occur at the end of 1968. He would go to Bangkok for R&R in early January and be home on January 28th., 1969. Like Jack's decision to extend his first tour, he stayed to help his Army family fight but unlike that first decision, he didn't share it with his other family at home.

September 1968

Dear Mom and Dad,

Well I've got some good news, I finally made Sergeant. I made it the day I left Vietnam. That's a few more bucks to save. I'll be getting a 60-buck raise in December because I've been in the Army 2 years. Then I hope to have made Staff Sergeant by then so that that will be another $50. I'm also trying to get $30 pro pay per month.

There's a change, I'm now back in Delta Company instead of Recon. Lt. M (my old Recon leader) is now Delta Company Commander and he asked me to come to Delta Company. I also got another Bronze Star and the highest Vietnamese medal (the Vietnamese Cross of Gallantry with Palm Leaf's) for the action on May 4th. I've got a 17-man squad in Mike Platoon. I believe we will be going back to Loc Ninh in a short time. No sweat. I've got my old M-14 back instead of that jammy M-16 and I'll be home in 5 months and 1 day, this time to stay. I'll try to get to Ft. Knox or Ft. Benjamin Harrison in Indiana. I might even try to get Wright Air Force Base. All I can do is hope.

I guess school will be starting soon. Well tell the kids to work hard and do good. When does Jerri start? Things aren't the same as when I left. If they were, I would go another 6 months but they're not. A guy got a chess game from home and we are playing it now. We are now on Highway 13 just outside of Quan Loi and Lai Khe. We're supposed to go to Thu Duc, down by Saigon next. I'll be leaving on February 25th. It will be cold, but I guess I'll take the chance. I may be extending 3 months to be able to come home when it's warm.

How's Dad doing? Fine, I hope. Well I better get checking weapons. I hardly have any free time. So, tell everyone I said hello, even the next-door neighbors and Bill if he calls up. So, take care and don't worry.

Love,

Jack

TOAN THANG PHASE II

TRAPEZOID

THE BIG RED ONE continued Phase II of Operation TOAN THANG during late September, October, and November 1968, with reconnaissance-in-force (RIF) operations, night ambushes, civic action programs and intelligence activities.

In late September, intelligence reported enemy activity in the Trapezoid area, so called because of its physical shape. The area extends from the west side of Ben Cat northwestward to the Michelin Rubber Plantation.

The most significant contacts of the week-long operation took place when elements of the 1/18th and the 1 /28th engaged well-entrenched groups of North Vietnamese regulars in two separate incidents. The first of the two actions began when Company C, 18th Infantry surprised an unknown number of enemies as the unit was proceeding to a resupply point.

On 7 October, elements of the 2d Battalion. 16th Infantry discovered a large enemy basecamp and hospital complex. It contained 3,600 pounds of medical supplies, 1,100 concussion grenades, one-hundred and fifty 82mm mortar rounds, 50 Chicom grenades, 400 RPG-7 charges, 584 RPG-2 rounds, 2,000 rounds of AK-47 ammunition, 100 rounds of 60mm mortar, 400 RPG-7 boosters, six anti-tank mines, seventy-five 75mm recoilless rifle rounds, 102 RPG-7 rounds, six "38" Smith and Wesson pistols, 5,000 grenade fuses, 1,000 fuse lighters, 400 US rifle grenades, and numerous other supplies and equipment.

During the engagement 19 enemy bodies were found.[19]

FSPB JULIE: OCTOBER 18-26, 1968

ENEMY ACTIVITY HAD been noted in the northern section of the Division's area of operation, and in early October intelligence indicated the possibility of the presence of the 1st North Vietnamese Army Division in the vicinity of the Fishhook Area, Tong Le Chon, and immediately across the Cambodian border. On 18 October elements of the BIG RED ONE established Fire Support Patrol Bases (FSPB) Rita, Julie, and Dot in the area, from which reconnaissance-in-force and sweep operations were conducted to determine the presence of the enemy division. During the early evening hours of 26 October, the NVA again attacked but were easily beaten off. The suicide attempt on FSPB Julie took the lives of 128 enemy soldiers. US casualties numbered eight.

FSPB RITA: OCTOBER 31-NOVEMBER 1, 1968

ON THE MORNING of 30 October, the BIG RED ONE unit killed 42 enemy soldiers while sustaining five US wounded. At various times during the evening of 31 October and early morning hours of 1 November, reconnaissance fires were conducted. In defense of Fire Support Base Rita, 1,300 rounds of artillery direct fire were expended, 800 rounds of indirect artillery fire, between 50,000 and 60,000 rounds of .50 caliber, 478 rounds of 81mm mortar, and the beehive rounds of the 105 battery were used. In addition, countless rounds of M-16 fire tore into the enemy's ranks. In the initial search of the area, immediately in and around the wire itself, 27 NVA bodies, two AK-47 rifles, five RPG launchers and from 150 to 200 RPG rounds were found. Flyovers indicated a possible 400 to 500 bodies lying in the woods around the fire support base. Seventeen US soldiers were killed.[20]

You better like your Thanksgiving Day dinner "traditional." If not, what's the Army going to do with 650,000 pounds of turkey?

Traditional it will be, with a menu aimed to please, if not surprise: roast tom turkey with all the trimmings.

In U.S. Army messhalls around the world, the Nov. 28 dinner menu, with a few local variations, will look like this:

Shrimp Cocktail

Cocktail Sauce   Crisp Saltines

Roast Tom Turkey

Cornbread Dressing   Bread Dressing
Giblet Gravy   Cranberry Sauce
Glazed Sweet Potatoes   Mashed Potatoes

Buttered Peas

Assorted Relish Tray

Hot Parker House Rolls   Butter Patties

Mincemeat Pie   Pumpkin Pie with Whipped Cream

Fruit Cake

Hard Candy   Salted Nuts

Assorted Fresh Fruit

Coffee   Tea   Milk

Christmas Day dinner will be similar. The Army estimates that each holiday meal will require the following amounts of food to see that every American soldier away from home gets his holiday meal:

650,000 pounds of Turkey; 16,500 gallons of giblet gravy; 245,000 pounds of bread and cornbread dressing; 130,000 mincemeat and pumpkin pies; 182,000 pounds of mashed potatoes; and 81,000 cans of glazed sweet potatoes.

Of this total, 185,000 pounds of turkey will be served to Army members in Vietnam. In addition, the 1st Logistical Command in Vietnam reports that it is laying in an extra supply of turkey so that the traditional American Thanksgiving banquet can be offered to members of the Free World Forces serving in Vietnam. (ANF)

Thanksgiving 1968 menu sent home by Jack

December 3, 1968

Dear Mom and Dad,

Well things are going pretty hectic here. We've had some contact lately but not too bad. Well only 82 days at the max. left in this stinking hole. I've finally come to my senses about this place. It's all changed now. The place is getting like the states more and more. They screwed me probably on my E-6 promotion (nothing new).

I had a fight with the Sergeant Major. All the fun has gone out of the place. They want you to be stateside in the Army and it can't be done. I wouldn't (and you can quote me on this) extend one day past my deros and wouldn't spend one more day in this Army institution. Because that's all it is, a mental institution. This place (the Army) would drive you nuts. I'd rather be a bum than be in the Army for your work. Because that's all a man's in this for, to be a bum lifer.

I'm sorry I haven't written to you sooner, but they haven't given us much slack to write. We've gone so many places I couldn't even name. I'm finally seeing the light. The Army has done nothing but screwed me since I've been in so I can't wait to get out and start school seriously. I believe (Political Science) or an English major would be my bag. I've got 10 months to stay at Fort Jackson and with a little luck I could get a few credits there in Columbia, SC at U.S.C.

I bet you thought I lost the watch Dad got me.... Well the answer is NO.... the watch band broke on patrol...but I pin the watch on my collar. A few added attractions since I came back to Recon. No more helmets...just bush hats-while we are at NDP's (night defensive positions) or in the rear. We are the only ones to wear camouflage fatigues. I'll send you a few pictures when I get them. They are neat. The gook broads go crazy over them.

They screwed me on my R&R for Christmas, but I'll go in January and a 3-day pass also but after January, look out Jack is coming home to stay.

I wouldn't mind coming over here for a job, but they have to be kidding me if they ever want me to come back over here in the Army...HA...They'd be nuts.

Look, I've talked enough about my troubles. You're not trying to cover-up anything serious about your health. If there is anything I can't stand is not to be told. If there is anything seriously wrong, contact the Red Cross and if they won't let me go, I'll get there one way or another...via Russia or Sweden if I have to...HA HA.

It's good that you've lost a little weight, safer also. If I lose any more weight, I may get home a little sooner because the wind will blow me there. My main meal is cigarettes. This food makes me sick. The pigs in the mess hall don't cook it, they spoil it. HA HA (short, 82 days).

But that good cooking of yours (WOW). How's Dad doing? Not working too hard, is he? Tell him to take it easy and don't let those punk bosses screw him up.

Well I've got my reassignment for back in the states. Guess...Ft. Jackson. South Carolina. Not Ft. Polk. HA HA. I finally screwed the Army. Well no big thing, they'll get me later again. No seriously, an NCO hasn't gotten too much trouble in Ft. Jackson because I'll be on a Committee Group and tell the trainees my war stories from 8 to 5 every day. Then I'm off. I'll have my own apartment off post. I'm thinking seriously of enrolling in evening classes at University of South Carolina.

Right now, I am platoon Sergeant for Recon platoon again. They requested I go back so I did. So, my address is Recon Echo Camp, 1st BN 18th Infantry (but not for long, short 81 days and wake up). HA HA, F.T.A. (F___ the Army).

Wow I have a bad attitude today. Too many men are getting hurt and killed because of some of these chicken-assed no-count Lieutenants, Captains, Majors, and Colonels over here (well might as well put Generals too). HA HA, no slack.

Tell Judy to learn to tie her shoelaces and I know Jim and Jeff just 'love' school, HA HA. Just like their big brother. HA HA. Hell, it will be too damn cold for me to do anything when I get home, but I won't care. So, Jerri is pushing on. It won't be long before she will be graduating. She and John will make a lovely couple, HA HA. Tell John I'll be waiting for him. Tell Bill F. and Bill M. I said hello and I'll drop by to see them when I get home.

Well it's getting dark and hard to see. So, take care and don't worry cause Jack the Sprat is coming home. Short. F.T.A.

Love, Jack

P.S. Tell everyone I said hello. What kind of car should I get? A Firebird or a Road Runner?

Jack in bush hat and Bronze Star Medal

December 1968

Dear Mom and Dad,

I'm just sending a few things we did that were in the paper. How's the Christmas spirit coming? Good, I hope.

Time is passing. 76 days and it won't be long before I'm home again.

Take care and don't worry.

Love,

Jack

Holiday dinner in the field

December 20, 1968

Dear Mom and Dad,

Well I've finally got some good news. I'll be home January 28th instead of February 24th. I got a drop so look for me to call around then from Oakland, California or McGuire Air Force base in New Jersey then.

My last day in the field is January 1st or December 31st. I have an R&R to Bangkok Thailand on January 8th. Also, my E-6 orders will probably be coming in, so they tell me I'll be wearing my Sergeant stripes when I come home. Wow, if I could get Staff Sergeant before I come home, I'd have the world by the tail when I get to Fort Jackson. I wouldn't have anything to do except tell people what to do (HA HA) and get the lifers mad.

We got hit the other night and all our gear was destroyed by a fire. Did you all have a nice Christmas? I hope so. This is the 20th today and the 23rd I'm going out until after Christmas to pull ambushes and patrol. This place we are at now is really bad. We can't even get enough water to drink let alone to wash.

It won't be too long. 38 days at the max and 10 days in the field (FTA). We can't stand it out here. It's a bad bag. Too much stateside harassment. That damn Johnson and that peace conference. When I get back, I'll be the biggest dissenter of them all. This is the silliest thing the US has ever done since the Bay of Pigs invasion. The Democrat asses. The big wigs are playing games, but they forget people are dying and getting hurt because of their games.

There's not much more so I'll be home. So, tell everyone I said hello and tell everyone Merry Christmas and Happy New Year. So, take care and I'll be home.

Love.

Jack

CHAPTER NINE
FEBRUARY 1969

JACK COMES HOME

Jack started 1969 in Vietnam. He wrote in his last letter, sent December 20, 1968, "Well I've finally got some good news. I'll be home January 28th instead of February 24th.. I have an R&R to Bangkok Thailand on January 8th. My last day in the field is January 1st or December 31st." Thus, our parents expected him home in late January 1969.

But a telegram arrived early in February, with news that Jack was killed in a firefight on February 2 near LAI KHE VIETNAM on February 2 1968. I remember that day, not realizing at the time, the world changed and life would be much different. Our parents were devastated, withdrawing into themselves. The family seemed to disintegrate as we each tried to understand what was happening. Jack's life, service and death still affect us over 50 years later and his scholarship and story will help students in the future. Perhaps he extended his tour in order to leave Vietnam when it would be warm back home. I believe the most likely reason was that Jack did not want to leave his Army comrades under his command. I imagine Jack being a good leader since he matured as a warrior. He knew how those under his command felt and did not expect anything more than he would give.

The Distinguished Service Cross citation best described how Jack was killed:

Staff Sergeant Freppon distinguished himself by exceptionally valorous actions on 2 February 1969 as a squad leader for a platoon which was conducting a reconnaissance-in-force mission near Lai Khe. Sergeant Freppon was serving as point man when he was suddenly pinned to the ground by fragmentation and rocket-propelled grenades and automatic weapons fire from well-concealed North Vietnamese Army troops. Fearing that his men would be trapped by the devastating hostile fire, he stood up to warn them of the entrenched enemy. Then, with complete disregard for his safety, he charged through the fusillade toward a North Vietnamese bunker. Although he was wounded repeatedly, he continued his assault on the fortification. He succeeded in destroying the bunker and was stopped only when he was mortally wounded by an enemy rocket-propelled grenade. His courage and self-sacrifice prevented many of his comrades from being killed or wounded. Staff Sergeant Freppon's extraordinary heroism and devotion to duty, at the cost of his life, were in keeping with the highest traditions of the military service and reflect great credit upon himself, his unit, and the United States Army.

Staff Sergeant John (Jack) Freppon died fighting the enemy in combat, heroically, in a Vietnam jungle on February 2, 1969.

western union

522P EST FEB 4 69 A409 LA274

L WAQ4S XV GOVT PD FAX WASHINGTON DC 4 237P EST

MR AND MRS JACK D FREPPON, DONT PHONE CHECK DLY CHGS ABOVE

75 CTS DONT DLR BTW 10PM AND 6 AM

1479 CLOVERNOLL DR CIN

THE SECRETARY OF THE ARMY HAS ASKED ME TO EXPRESS HIS DEEP
REGRET THAT YOUR SON STAFF SERGEANT JOHN D FREPPON DIED IN
VIETNAM ON 2 FEB 69 AS A RESULT OF WOUNDS RECEIVED WHILE ON
A COMBAT OPERATION WHEN ENGAGED A HOSTILE FORCE IN A FIREFIGHT
PLEASE ACCEPT MY DEEPEST SYMPATHY. THIS CONFIRMS PERSONAL NOTIFICATION
MADE BY A REPRESENTATIVE OF THE SECRETARY OF THE ARMY
KENNETH G WICKHAM MAJOR GENERAL USA F19 THE ADJUTANT GENERAL
(519).

CHAPTER TEN
TRIBUTES

Jack's comrades shared memories and condolences on his death in combat.

Several Army Generals and a couple of politicians sent letters expressing their condolences about Jack's death. Four of his mates also described serving with him.

He enlisted since he believed he would help the South Vietnamese people stop the spread of Communism from the North. I believe he relished the adventure. He was a good soldier who volunteered for ambush patrols, listening and observation posts, and point duty. He helped his fellow war buddies even though some questioned his desire to keep his weapons clean or digging fox holes when it seemed unnecessary but then jumping into the holes to save their lives.

Jack was a courageous leader. He cared about his troops. He fought alongside them, commanded them, humored them, and ensured they had enough food and water even when he had to give some of his up for them. I wish I would have gotten to know Jack better and would have attempted to compose his story sooner. I hope this book complements his service and helps all who read it to learn more about the war and someone who died fighting in Vietnam.

A buddy's comment, "Jack was too brave for his own good," pretty much summed up how Jack served.

LETTER FROM UNITED STATES ARMY GENERAL WESTMORELAND

WASHINGTON

6 February 1969

Dear Mr. and Mrs. Freppon:

Please know that the thoughts of many are with you at this time. The passing of your son, Staff Sergeant John D. Freppon, on 2 February, in Vietnam is a great loss not only for his fellow soldiers but for his country as well.

I know that words can do little to relieve your grief just now, but I hope that you will find comfort in the knowledge that through your son's sacrifice he will live in the hearts of all men who desire peace and freedom.

As our Nation strives to overcome those whose ultimate aim is to deny other men the blessings of freedom and human dignity which we hold dear, the most distressing thing we have to face is the loss of young men such as your son. It is through their devoted service and courage that our country can remain strong and our purpose steadfast.

All members of the Army join me in expressing our deepest sympathy to you.

Sincerely,

W. C. WESTMORELAND
General, United States Army
Chief of Staff

Mr. and Mrs. Jack D. Freppon
1479 Clovernoll Drive
Cincinnati, Ohio 45231

LETTER FROM STANLEY R. RESOR, SECRETARY OF THE ARMY

SECRETARY OF THE ARMY
WASHINGTON

February 12, 1969

Dear Mr. and Mrs. Freppon:

Please accept my deepest sympathy for the death of your son, Staff Sergeant John D. Freppon, in Vietnam on February 2, 1969.

We are proud of his military accomplishments and grateful to him for his contribution to our Nation's strength. All members of the United States Army join me in expressing the hope that the memory of his dedicated service will help to ease your sorrow.

Sincerely yours,

Stanley R. Resor

Mr. and Mrs. Jack D. Freppon
1479 Clovernoll Drive
Cincinnati, Ohio 45231

LETTER FROM JAMES A. RHODES, GOVERNOR OF OHIO

THE STATE OF OHIO
OFFICE OF THE GOVERNOR
STATE HOUSE, COLUMBUS

JAMES A. RHODES
GOVERNOR

March 3, 1969

Mr. and Mrs. Jack D. Freppon
1479 Clovernoll Drive
Cincinnati, Ohio 45231

Dear Mr. and Mrs. Freppon:

Through the Adjutant General of Ohio I have just learned that the casualty list released by the Department of Defense on February 5, 1969, carries the name of your son, SSG John D. Freppon.

Words cannot express the depth of my personal sympathy and the concern and sympathy of all Ohio citizens for the parents and families of men who have given their lives in Vietnam in defense of human liberty.

We join our prayers with you and your neighbors that the consolations of your faith may bless and comfort you in this time of sorrow.

Sincerely,

JAMES A. RHODES
Governor

JAR:mh

LETTER FROM PRESIDENT
RICHARD M. NIXON

THE WHITE HOUSE

WASHINGTON

February 15, 1969

Dear Mr. and Mrs. Freppon:

It was with profound regret that I learned of the death
of your son, Staff Sergeant John D. Freppon.

I realize the great sorrow you have been called upon
to bear. It is my sincere hope that you will gain con-
solation from the memory of your son's unselfish
dedication to our free world at a critical time when
brave and dependable men were so urgently needed.
Our country is grateful for your son's contribution to
the cause of freedom.

Mrs. Nixon joins me in extending to you our sincere
sympathy and you may be sure you will remain in our
prayers.

Sincerely,

Richard Nixon

Mr. and Mrs. Jack D. Freppon
1479 Clovernoll Drive
Cincinnati, Ohio

LETTER FROM UNITED STATES ARMY
MAJOR GENERAL ORWIN C. TALBOTT

DEPARTMENT OF THE ARMY
HEADQUARTERS 1ST INFANTRY DIVISION
Office of the Commanding General
APO San Francisco 96345

21 FEB 1969

Mr. & Mrs. Jack D. Freppon
1479 Clovernoll Drive
Cincinnati, Ohio 45231

Dear Mr. & Mrs. Freppon:

The officers and men of the 1st Infantry Division join with me in extending our deepest and most sincere sympathy in the loss of your son, John.

Your son served his nation proudly, carrying out a tradition of duty to country that is a cherished part of our American heritage. He was an outstanding soldier, and his devotion to duty earned him the highest respect of members of the division.

Realizing that my words can scarcely compensate for your loss, I trust that in some small measure I can ease your burden of grief by assuring you that John served his country well. He was a fine man, and we of the 1st Infantry Division mourn the death of a valued comrade.

As soldiers we believe that the Creator of all men reserves a special place in His Kingdom for those who pay the supreme sacrifice for the cause of freedom and our way of life. It is my hope that your faith, your family, and your friends will help you in this hour of need.

Sincerely,

ORWIN C. TALBOTT
Major General, USA

LETTER FROM UNITED STATES ARMY
GENERAL CREIGHTON W. ABRAMS

HEADQUARTERS
UNITED STATES MILITARY ASSISTANCE COMMAND, VIETNAM
OFFICE OF THE COMMANDER
APO SAN FRANCISCO 96222

2 6 FEB 1969

Mr. and Mrs. Jack D. Freppon
1479 Clovernoll Drive
Cincinnati, Ohio 45231

Dear Mr. and Mrs. Freppon:

On behalf of the U. S. Military Assistance Command, Vietnam, I wish
to extend my sympathy to you over the loss of your son, Staff Sergeant
John D. Freppon, United States Army, and express my condolences during your time of sorrow and bereavement.

It is my hope that you will find a measure of solace in knowing your
son gave his life for a noble cause, the defense of liberty in the free
world. Rest assured that we who remain here in Vietnam will continue
our efforts to bring peace to this troubled land so that your son's sacrifice will not have been in vain.

Sincerely,

CREIGHTON W. ABRAMS
General, United States Army
Commanding

LETTERS FROM THOSE WHO SERVED WITH JACK

Mr. and Mrs. Freppon,

I'm sending this card and letter to express how sorry I am to hear about your son being killed in Vietnam.

I used to be a medic in his Platoon in D Company 1ˢᵗ and 18ᵗʰ. He was one of the nicest guys I ever knew.

I learned of this death in the Army Times. It hurt to see it, but it didn't surprise me. We all asked Jack not to extend. He always walked point. He was too brave for his own good.

There aren't many things I can say except that I am sorry and tell you Jack was respected and liked by every man in the company.

Sincerely, R.C.

March 29, 1969

Dear Mr. and Mrs. Freppon

I received your letter and was more than glad to hear from you. Mrs. Freppon, speaking of your deceased son, he was one of the best soldiers that I have ever met. Many times, Jack and I sat around and talked of home. He told me personally before he went on R&R that he was going home because I told him how good that his day had arrived for him to return home after serving 18 months over here. He was supposed to be stationed at Fort Jackson in South Carolina and I told him that it was a very nice place and he accepted it from me with thanks but a few days later he and I were sitting around talking and he told me he was going to extend. I, Mrs. Freppon, am a Negro soldier and a good friend of your son and told him to go home but he told me that he had made up his mind to extend for the early out. So, he returned to his unit which was Recon platoon. Mrs. Freppon, your son really cared about the men he was serving with and all of us got along just like brothers. He was very proud of the unit he was serving with which is the First Infantry Division better known as the Big Red One to us. When I came to Vietnam I volunteered to be assigned to Recon and there I met Jack which was in May of 1968 and he began teaching me about the kind of operations that we have to go on and again I thank him very much because what I learned from him as my Squad Leader and Platoon Sergeant really helped me a lot. Mrs. Freppon, I realized that I haven't answered too many of your questions but me and my friend have decided to visit you personally on our return home if the good Lord is willing. My home is in South Carolina, 91 miles south of where Jack was supposed to go. Mr. and Mrs. Freppon, I know that it was a sad thing to hear about your son but just like you said in your letter, it was God's will, so God bless you all.

From: P.F.C. Jesse G.

Dear Mr. & Mrs. Freppon,

Before I go any further, I would like to express my deepest sympathy for you and your family. I sincerely hope that by the time you finish this letter, some of your questions will be answered and some of the pain eased.

At the time of your son's death, I was not present. I myself was already hospitalized. I was injured in January and did not get a chance to talk to Jack after that. Up until that time we were very close. We talked seriously about several things. By my being a Negro the racial issue came up several times but mostly we talked about the war.

I remember one day Jack and I played football with an empty soda can. We had a ball too. Your son was indeed a fine person. Some of the fellows would not associate because of the color of my skin and many times Jack has told them that between us there could be no misunderstandings.

Together Jack and I had become very bitter about the way we were being treated and the food we had to eat. Several times we had missed meals. There is something you mentioned in your letter about Jack becoming discouraged and giving up. I believe this to be true.

I will try, myself and a friend, to pay at least a short visit to you and your family.

Now I must close my letter and want very much to thank you for your letter. So now I must say good-bye and God Bless. I pray for Jack often.

Mr. and Mrs. Freppon your son was a grand fellow, and may God bless you all.

Sincerely, Sgt. R.

April 3, 1969

Dear Mrs. Freppon,

I was one of your son's friends in the Recon platoon. I transferred however after Jack's death, so I didn't know how to contact you until I visited the platoon a few days ago.

I want to tell you how truly sorry I am for the unfortunate and untimely death of your son. Please accept my sincere and heartfelt condolences.

Jack set an honorable example for every man in the platoon and I always tried to emulate his leadership qualities. Jack's men always came first, and his affairs were put aside until he knew all the men were prepared and had the things they needed. He would never ask his men to do something he could do himself and he went against traditional Army routine by working and associating freely with his associates.

Every man respected him, and he had many Vietnamese friends as well as GI's. It was not hard to be Jack's friend, and everyone knew him as a modest man but always being able to cheer men up when they needed it. A smile was always a prominent feature of his appearance and his loss deprived all of us of a great man, a man to be loved and respected and most of all, remembered.

I hope your grief has been subdued by the knowledge that the Lord has taken the best of care of the man whom we all knew and loved.

Very truly yours, W.M.

A TRUE AMERICAN HERO

SSG Freppon, thank you for your sacrifice, leadership and bravery. You sacrificed so others could live, thinking of your men, versus yourself.

As a fellow Madisonville, Purcell Grad, and Big Red One soldier, I couldn't be more proud of you. While stationed in DC, I visited the wall often, and I left you one of my commanders coins in appreciation of your service. As a scout, I hope to see you at Fiddlers Green someday.

Colonel Todd Mayer

Posted on 4.14.2015 at the Wall of Faces
https://www.vvmf.org/Wall-of-Faces/17224/John-D-Freppon/

CHAPTER ELEVEN
CITATIONS AND AWARDS

Jack was awarded numerous citations and medals for gallantry and heroism while serving, fighting and dying in Vietnam. It is an impressive collection, receiving among others, 2 Purple Hearts and the Distinguished Service Cross. I included medal citations I could find and requirements for other awards he earned in battle. Jack did not seem to care about the medals and awards but was motivated and encouraged by commanders who provided battle support to accomplish missions. When I read what Jack did to earn those honors, there is the consistent theme of a brave warrior who was willing to sacrifice himself in battle to help save the lives of comrades.

The medals will be framed in a case at his alma mater high school.

DISTINGUISHED SERVICE CROSS

Awarded for Actions During Vietnam War

Service: Army *Rank:* Sergeant

Division: 1st Infantry Division

Date of action: 2 February 1969

CITATION:

For extraordinary heroism in connection with military operations involving conflict with an armed hostile force in the Republic of Vietnam, while serving with Company E, 1st Battalion, 18th Infantry, 2nd Brigade, 1st Infantry Division. Staff Sergeant Freppon distinguished himself by exceptionally valorous actions on 2 February 1969 as a squad leader for a platoon which was conducting a reconnaissance-in-force mission near Lai Khe.

Sergeant Freppon was serving as point man when he was suddenly pinned to the ground by fragmentation and rocket-propelled grenades and automatic weapons fire from well-concealed North Vietnamese Army troops.

Fearing that his men would be trapped by the devastating hostile fire, he stood up to warn them of the entrenched enemy. Then, with complete disregard for his safety, he charged through the fusillade toward a North Vietnamese bunker.

Although he was wounded repeatedly, he continued his assault on the fortification. He succeeded in destroying the bunker and was stopped only when he was mortally wounded by an enemy rocket-propelled grenade. His courage and self-sacrifice prevented many of his comrades from being killed or wounded.

Staff Sergeant Freppon's extraordinary heroism and devotion to duty, at the cost of his life, were in keeping with the highest traditions of the military service and reflect great credit upon himself, his unit, and the United States Army.

SILVER STAR

Awarded for Actions During Vietnam War

Service: Army *Rank:* First Class

Division: 1st Infantry Division

Date of Action: 30 October 1967

CITATION:

For gallantry in action against a hostile force while serving with Company D, 1st Battalion, 18th Infantry Regiment, 1st Infantry Division on 30 October 1967 in the Republic of Vietnam.

During Operation SHENANDOAH II, Private First Class Freppon was serving as a rifleman on a search and destroy mission near Loc Ninh.

His unit was moving in a large rubber plantation when they were engaged by a large Viet Cong force using hand grenades, machine guns, and automatic weapons. Machine gun fire emanating from a Viet Cong bunker was inflicting heavy casualties on the friendly force.

As his comrades provided covering fire, PFC Freppon began to maneuver against the enemy bunker. He was nearing the complex when he was spotted and taken under fire by the insurgents.

With complete disregard for his personal safety, Private First Class Freppon charged forward and overran the bunker. He succeeded in killing the three Viet Cong manning the machine gun and captured valuable equipment.

Ignoring relentless enemy fire from other positions, he continued to move forward and place deadly fire onto the insurgents. This enabled the remainder of his company to advance and subsequently rout the hostile force.

His bold initiative and dauntless courage significantly contributed to the overwhelming defeat of the Viet Cong and he was undoubtedly responsible for saving the lives of several fellow soldiers.

Private First Class Freppon's unquestionable valor in close combat against numerically superior hostile forces is in keeping with the finest traditions of the military service and reflects great credit upon himself, the 1st Infantry Division, and the United States Army.

BRONZE STAR MEDAL WITH "V" DEVICE

Awarded for Actions During Vietnam War

Service: Army *Rank:* Specialist

Division: 1ˢᵗ Infantry Division

Date of action: 4 May 1968

CITATION:

For heroism not involving partici-pation in aerial flight, in connection with military operations against a hostile force in the Republic of Viet-nam:

On this date, Specialist Freppon was serving as a rifleman with his bat-talion reconnaissance platoon on an operation northeast of Di An. As the friendly force proceeded along a creek, it was suddenly Subjected to intense fire from enemy spider holes along the banks.

With complete disregard for his per-sonal safety, Specialist Freppon vol-untarily maneuvered through the hail of hostile rounds along the bank and killed several Viet Cong.

Observing several insurgents retreating across an open rice paddy, he pursued them and received heavy enemy fire from a tree line. He engaged the Viet Cong with a devastating barrage which killed several of the withdrawing insurgents.

His exemplary courage and bold determination contributed significantly to the successful outcome of the encounter. Spe-cialist Four Freppon's outstanding display of aggressiveness, devotion to duty, and personal bravery is in keeping with the finest traditions of the military service and reflects great credit upon himself, the 1ˢᵗ Infantry Division, and the United States Army.

BRONZE STAR MEDAL

Awarded for Actions During Vietnam War

Service: Army *Rank:* Sergeant

Division: 1ˢᵗ Infantry Division

Date of action: 21 October 1968

CITATION:

For heroism not involving participation in aerial flight, in connection with military operations against a hostile force in the Republic of Vietnam:

On this date, Sergeant Freppon was serving as a squad Leader with his company on a reconnaissance in force operation. As the friendly unit proceeded through a treacherous area, contact was made with a numerically superior enemy force.

With complete disregard for his personal safety, Sergeant Freppon maneuvered through a hail of hostile rounds from man to man to direct their movement and fire on the insurgents.

He continued to brave the aggressor barrages and adjusted his element's suppressive covering fire which enabled another squad to assault and overrun the enemy position.

His courageous initiative and bold determination significantly contributed to the successful accomplishment of his unit's mission.

Sergeant Freppon's outstanding displays of aggressiveness, devotion to duty, and personal bravery is in keeping with the finest traditions of the military service and reflects great credit upon himself, the 1st Infantry Division, and the United States Army.

SOLDIER'S MEDAL

Awarded for Actions During Vietnam War

Service: Army *Rank:* Sergeant

Division: 1st Infantry Division

Date of action: 25 November 1968

CITATION:

For heroism at the risk of life not involving conflict with an armed enemy in the Republic of Vietnam on 25 November 1968.

On this date, Sergeant Freppon was serving as a squad leader with his unit's reconnaissance platoon when it engaged a Viet Cong force in the vicinity of Bien Hoa.

Helicopter gunships were called in to provide fire support. During their first pass, one of the aircraft crashed.

As Sergeant Freppon began moving toward the downed helicopter, it burst into flames, igniting ammunition and rockets.

With complete disregard for his personal safety, he rushed forward and began pulling the injured crew from the burning craft.

Despite the nearby explosion of munitions, Sergeant Freppon remained at the crash site and assisted in administering emergency treatment to the casualties until they were ready to be moved to a landing zone for aerial evacuation.

His exemplary courage and selfless concern for the welfare of his comrades were instrumental in saving several friendly lives. Staff Sergeant Freppon's heroic actions are in keeping with the highest traditions of the military service and reflect great credit upon himself, the 1st Infantry Division, and the United States Army.

ARMY COMMENDATION MEDAL

Awarded for Actions During Vietnam War

Service: Army

Division: 1st Infantry Division

The Army Commendation Medal is awarded to any member of the Armed Forces of the United States other than General Officers who, while serving in any capacity with the Army after

6 December 1941, distinguished himself by heroism, meritorious achievement or meritorious service. Award may be made to a member of the Armed Forces of a friendly foreign nation who, after 1 June 1962, distinguishes himself by an act of heroism, extraordinary achievement, or meritorious service which has been of mutual benefit to a friendly nation and the United States.

ARMY GOOD CONDUCT MEDAL

Awarded for Actions During Vietnam War

Service: Army

Division: 1st Infantry Division

The Good Conduct Medal is awarded for exemplary behavior, efficiency, and fidelity in active Federal Military service. It is awarded on a selective basis to each soldier who distinguishes himself from among his/her fellow soldiers by their exemplary conduct, efficiency, and fidelity throughout a specified period of continuous enlisted active Federal military service. Qualifying periods of service include each three years completed after 27 August 1940 or, for first award only, upon completion of at least one year upon termination of service if separated prior to three years. The immediate commander must approve the award and the award must be announced in permanent orders.

NATIONAL DEFENSE SERVICE MEDAL

Awarded for Actions During Vietnam War

Service: Army

Division: 1st Infantry Division

The National Defense Service Medal was awarded for honorable active service for any period between 27 June 1950 and 27 July 1954, between 1 January 1961 and 14 August 1974, and between 2 August 1990 and 30 November 1995, and from 11 September 2001 to a date to be determined. For the purpose of the award, the following persons will not be considered as performing active service: (1) Guard and Reserve forces personnel on short tours of duty to fulfill training obligations under an inactive duty training program. (2) Any person on active duty for the sole purpose of undergoing a physical examination. (3) Any person on temporary active duty to serve on boards, courts, commissions and like organizations or on active duty for purposes other than extended active duty. b. The National Defense Service Medal may be awarded to members of the Reserve Components who are ordered to Federal active duty, regardless of duration, except for the categories listed above. Any member of the Guard or Reserve who, after 31 December 1960, becomes eligible for the Armed Forces Expeditionary Medal, Vietnam Service Medal or the Southwest Asia Service Medal is also eligible for the National Defense Service Medal.

PURPLE HEART

Awarded for Actions During Vietnam War

Service: Army

Division: 1st Infantry Division

The Purple Heart is awarded in the name of the President of the United States to any member of an Armed Force who, while serving with the U.S. Armed Services after 5 April 1917, has been wounded or killed, or who has died or may hereafter die after being wounded;

(1) In any action against an enemy of the United States;

(2) In any action with an opposing armed force of a foreign country in which the Armed Forces of the United States are or have been engaged;

(3) While serving with friendly foreign forces engaged in an armed conflict against an opposing armed force in which the United States is not a belligerent party;

(4) As a result of an act of any such enemy of opposing armed forces;

(5) As the result of an act of any hostile foreign force;

(6) After 28 March 1973, as a result of an international terrorist attack against the United States or a foreign nation friendly to the United States, recognized as such an attack

by the Secretary of the department concerned, or jointly by the Secretaries of the departments concerned if persons from more than one department are wounded in the attack; or,

(7) After 28 March 1973, as a result of military operations, while serving outside the territory of the United States as part of a peacekeeping force.

(8) After 7 December 1941, by weapon fire while directly engaged in armed conflict, regardless of the fire causing the wound.

(9) While held as a prisoner of war or while being taken captive. b. A wound for which the award is made must have required treatment by a medical officer.

AWARDED 2 PURPLE HEARTS

VIETNAM GALLANTRY CROSS WITH PALM

Awarded for Actions During Vietnam War

Service: Army

Division: 1st Infantry Division

Awarded by the Vietnam Government to military personnel who have accomplished deeds of valor or displayed heroic conduct while fighting the enemy and have been cited individually at the regiment, brigade, division, corps, or armed forces level.

VIETNAM MILITARY MERIT MEDAL

Awarded for Actions During Vietnam War

Service: Army

Division: 1st Infantry Division

The highest military decoration bestowed to enlisted personnel by the Republic of Vietnam during the years of the Vietnam War.to Allied Non-Commissioned Officers and Enlisted Men for valor while fighting the enemy in the Republic of Vietnam.

Servicemen of courage and rare self-sacrifice, they displayed at all times, the most tactful cooperation while aiding the Armed Forces of the Republic of Vietnam to repel the Red wave undermining South Vietnam and Southeast Asia. With a ready zeal and commendable response, they fought on to the end in every mission and set a brilliant example for their fellow soldiers. They died in the performance of duty. Behind them they leave the abiding grief of their former comrades-in-arms, Vietnamese and American.

VIETNAM SERVICE MEDAL

Awarded for Actions During Vietnam War

Service: Army

Division: 1ˢᵗ Infantry Division

Awarded to all members of the Armed Forces of the United

States serving in Vietnam and contiguous waters or airspace thereover, after 3 July 1965 through 28 March 1973. Members of the Armed Forces of the United States in Thailand, Laos, or Cambodia, or the airspace thereover, during the same period and serving in direct support of operations in Vietnam are also eligible for this award. To be eligible for award of the medal, individual must:

(1) Be attached to or regularly serve for one or more days with an organization participating in or directly supporting military operations; or

(2) Be attached to or regularly serve for one or more days aboard a naval vessel directly supporting military operations; or

(3) Actually participate as a crewmember in one or more aerial flights into airspace above Vietnam and contiguous waters directly supporting military operations; or

(4) Serve on temporary duty for 30 consecutive days or 60 nonconsecutive days in Vietnam or contiguous areas, except that the time limit may be waived for personnel participating in actual combat operations. Individuals qualified for the

Armed Forces Expeditionary Medal for service in Vietnam between 1 July 1958 and 3 July 1965 shall remain qualified for the medal. Upon request, the individual may be awarded the Vietnam Service Medal in lieu of the Armed Forces Expeditionary Medal. In such instances, the Armed Forces Expeditionary Medal will be deleted from the list of authorized medals in the individual's personnel records.

VIETNAM CAMPAIGN MEDAL

Awarded for Actions During Vietnam War

Service: Army

Division: 1st Infantry Division

The Republic of Vietnam Campaign Medal is awarded to personnel who meet one of the following requirements:

a. Served in the Republic of Vietnam for six months during the period of 1 March 1961 and 28 March 1973.

b. Served outside the geographical limits of the Republic of Vietnam and contributed direct combat support to the Republic of Vietnam and Armed Forces for six months. Such individuals must meet the criteria established for the Armed Forces Expeditionary Medal (for Vietnam) or the Vietnam Service Medal, to qualify for the Republic of Vietnam Campaign Medal.

c. Six months service is not required for individuals who were wounded by hostile forces; killed in action or otherwise in line of duty; or captured by hostile forces.

IN MEMORIAM OF A HERO

IN MEMORIAM OF A HERO

YOUR SERVICEMAN

Posthumous Honors Given Seven

Gen. Roper, left, Mr. and Mrs. Freppon, Mr. and Mrs. O'Banion, Mr. and Mrs. Murray, Mrs. Secrees and son, and Mrs. Moore and daughter.

John D. Freppon
. . . graduate of Purcell

Local Youth, Two-Tour Vet, Dies In Vietnam

S. Sgt. John D. Freppon, 20, son of Mr. and Mrs. Jack D. Freppon, 1479 Clovernoll Dr., College Hill, was killed in Vietnam Sunday, the Defense Department said. He had nearly completed his second tour of duty there.

Mrs. Freppon said the family received word Tuesday of the death. She said she didn't know exactly where in Vietnam he was stationed at the time. She said she had expected her son to have completed his tour in Vietnam January 28.

Sergeant Freppon was a 1966 graduate of Purcell High School and attended the University of Cincinnati. He was a winner of the Purple Heart and the Silver and Bronze Star Medals.

He is also survived by two sisters, Geraldine and Judith Freppon and two brothers, Jeffrey and James Freppon, all at home.

ADDENDA

LAI KHE AREA RUBBER PLANTATION AND VIETNAM WAR BUNKERS

2013 VISIT TO VIETNAM

ORIGINAL LETTERS HOME FROM JACK

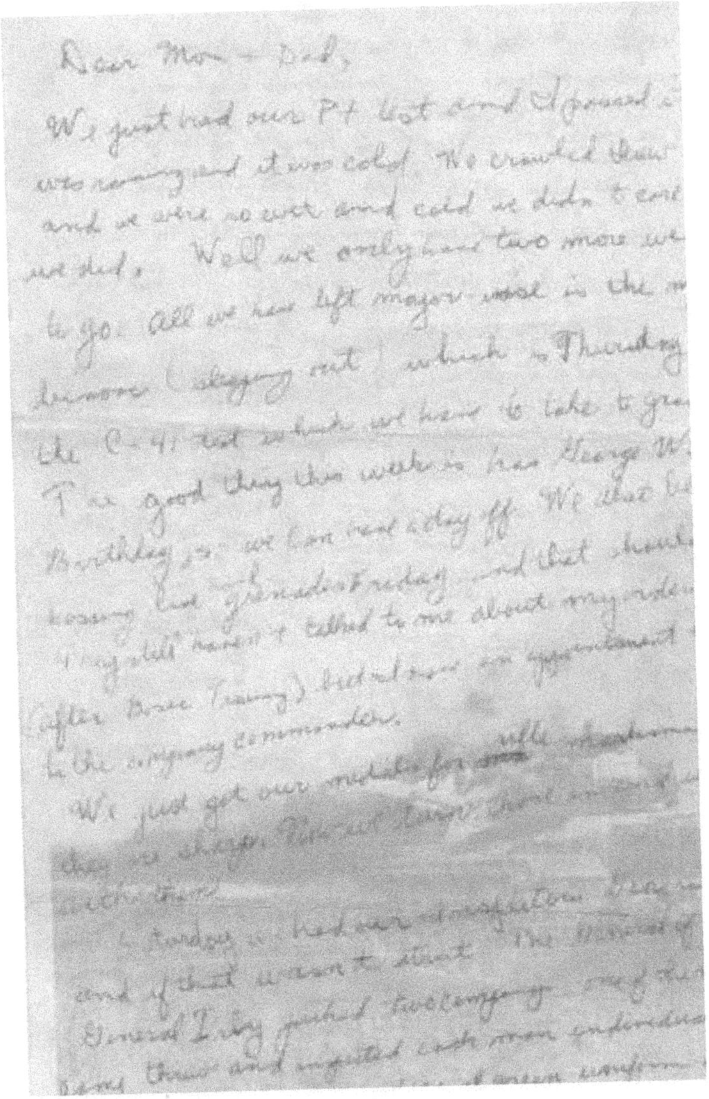

Dear Mom – Dad,

We just had our PT test and I passed it
was raining and it was cold. We crawled [illegible]
and we were so wet and cold we didn't care
we did. Well we only have two more we[illegible]
to go. All we have left major [illegible] is the [illegible]
[illegible] (shipping out) which is Thursday
the C-41 test which we have to take to gra[illegible]
The good thing this week is has George W[illegible]
Birthday so we have a day off. We [illegible]
[illegible] grenade test today and that should
[illegible] talked to me about my orders
after Basic Training) but [illegible] appointment
to the company commander.
We just got our medals for rifle marksman[illegible]
they are cheap. [illegible]
with them.
Saturday we had our inspection [illegible]
and of that we went to [illegible]. The [illegible]
General [illegible] pushed two company [illegible]
came through and inspected each man individually
[illegible]

asked God to take me from this earth. It scar
my daylights out of me when those machine
started firing and those dynamite charges at
oing off. There was only one guy hurt. He
scared and stood up, he was wounded twice in
shoulders. They had trees in between the la
and these lots of the area which was quite
sight. We crawled under barbed wire and in
out of trenches

We should be graduating ~~~~ march 3rd
and should leave march 4 or 5th. If I don't
a leave, I don't think it'll be home for a
6 months if they send me to Colorado or Oklahoma
But I'm pretty sure I'll get a pass this
weekend if all goes well.

Things are looking up now. They're giving
more time to eat, better food, and more
soaps to eat.

The harassment is almost gone and
being treated right now. We get this
with they say AIT is bum compared to B
Training. So I can't wait till I get out of h

Dear Mom + Dad,

Well I just thought I'd just drop
line — or two
That's really weird about that weather
back in the state. That's too bad, August
and September are the best months. It's
a shame for it to be ruined by cold
weather. Watch when the kids get
school, the weather will be so nice
and it will get so hot, they won't be
able to stand it.
That's great about Jeff and what the
principle said. Tell Jim to behave
and obey the teacher and do well.
The school sounds pretty nice
and modern.
I wouldn't send any money through the
mail because they are censored, and
they're probably be a light figured some
of a gun would like it.
About those ambushes. They
do get crowded out in the
boonie sometimes. There was a
rumor about the First Division
moving to another location far
north but it will be around
next May or June.
About the ambushes, I plan
to go out on another this week

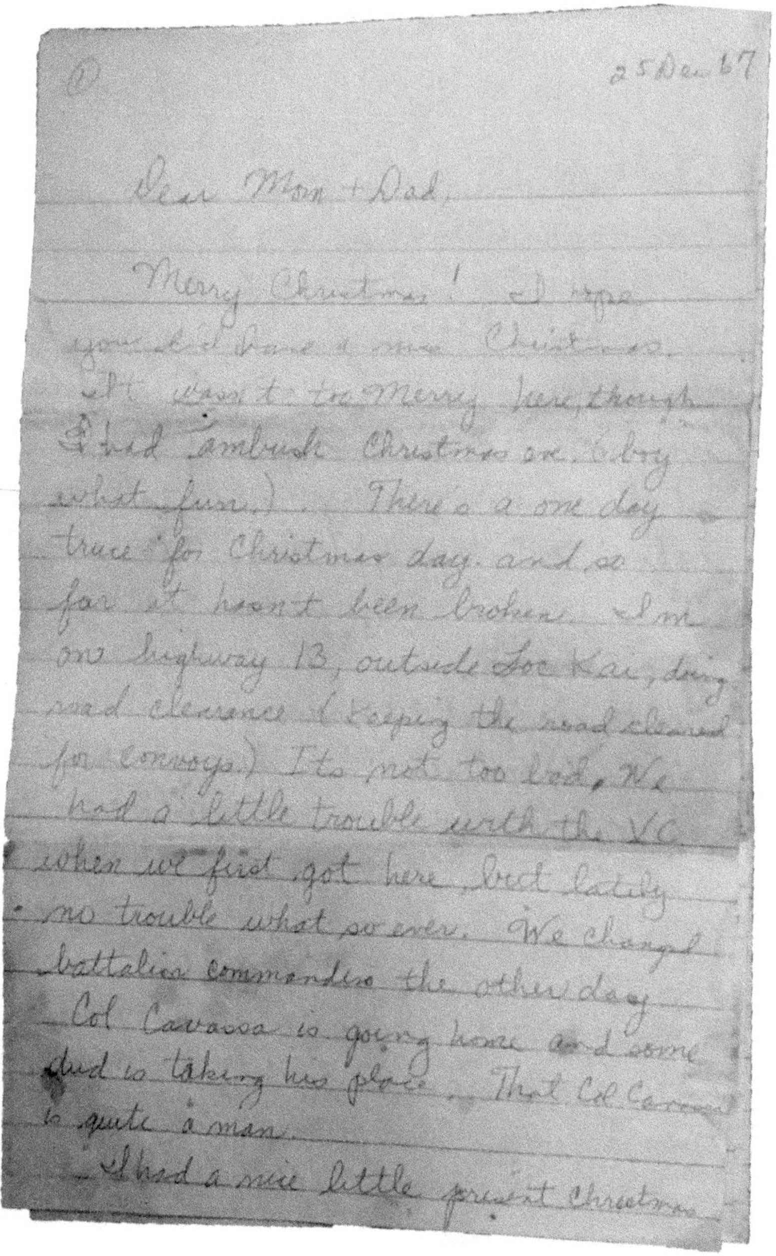

25 Dec 67

Dear Mom + Dad,

Merry Christmas! I hope you all have a nice Christmas. It wasn't too merry here, though I had ambush Christmas eve (boy what fun.) There's a one day truce for Christmas day and so far it hasn't been broken. I'm on highway 13, outside Loc Kai, doing road clearance (keeping the road cleared for convoys.) It's not too bad. We had a little trouble with the VC when we first got here, but lately no trouble whatsoever. We changed battalion commanders the other day. Col Cavassa is going home and some dud is taking his place. That Col Cavassa is quite a man.

I had a nice little present Christmas

FRI 13th Oct

Dear Mom + Dad,

Well I'm enjoying what I'm doing now. I've completed jump school. I am in the field at Phuc Vinn. and I tell you I've already seen enough action that I'll ever want to see. The first day we were there, we dug in. Thank God they didn't hit us that night, because we were digging in until 1:00 in the morning. Then we have guard at least three hours a night so we get around three hours a night to sleep. I tell you one thing I've never been so tired as I have been now.

Things are so bad here we can't even get 150 meters outside the perimeter without getting hit. Our battalion since we've been here, have lost 5 men. The 1st of the 2nd Inf (whom we relieved lost 42). We got hit the second night and bullets were flying all over the place. Shrapnel

Nov 9. 1967

Dear Mom + Dad,

I have to apologize for not writing in so long a time but this is alot different than my other job.

This is the first "rest" we've had in two months. Time is really going fast over here and I have to admit we've been in alot of action. We have been in 4 fire fights (battles) and killed around (and this is not an exaggeration) 1000 gooks. At Shennendoah Operation we wiped out two hundred of those pigs. We lost around 5 men which was the bad thing.

The first Infantry Div. is seeing the most action since the beginning of the war. The only thing, the rest of the battalions don't have their stuff together and I have to say, the VC are getting the best out of them. I can't say what units but last month one battalion was whipped so bad the man who was in charge of the battalion after the battle was a sargent. The battalion commander was killed, all the captains, lieutenants, and sargents E-6 and above.

And just 3 days ago another unit was hit. They lost 66 men and a battalion commander. The funny thing about the VC these days, is that they stay there and fight you instead of running away.

We were on Dogface hill, 3 thousand meters from Loc Nihn (where the VC overran last week) and I didn't think we'd make it out of there. They tried to overrun us. That's where they made their first mistake. There were bodies

Sept 26

Dear Mom and Dad,

Well I thought I'd just write a few lines since I haven't been too regular with my letters.

I'm still at Quan Loy but the rumor is that we will move either to Loc Kay which is to the south by Dian or to War Zone C, near the Black Virgin Mts, around 8 miles from here. If we move to the latter I think we will see our first action with the Viet Cong.

It doesn't matter much to me but I hope it is Loc Kay. Loc Kay is fairly nice. A nice village, a beach, modern conveniences.

This rain and dirt is really trying on your nerves. Your almost never clean and your boots stay wet almost all the time.

A good thing about it is that we get these sundries packs which we get all the cigerettes, candy, socks, and we get almost anything we need.

Guys who haven't obtained the art of proper physical hygiene are coming down with jungle rot and VD.

We usually eat two hot meals a day but when I'm

MAJOR BATTLES
1 MAY 67-31 DEC 68

NAME OF BATTLE	DATE	U.S. UNITS	ENEMY KILLED	LOCATION
	1968			
XOM BUNG	6 Jan	A Co 2/18 Inf; A, B Co 2/2 Mech.	100	30 miles N. Saigon
AN MY	1-2 Feb	Recon, A, C, D Co 1/28 Inf; B Troop ¼ Cav; D Troop ¼ Cav; Hq Plt B Troop ¼ Cav; A, B Co 2/16 Inf.	372	1 mile N. Phu Loi
XOM MOI I	2 Feb	A Troop ¼ Cav.	46	5 miles N Tan Son Nhut Air Base
TAN HIEP	4 May	D Co 1/18 Inf; Div Arty; A, B Troop ¼ Cav.	257	2 miles N. Di An
XOM MOI II	5 May	2d Plt B Co 1/18 Inf; A, B Troop ¼ Cav.	40	5 miles N. Tan Son Nhut Air Base
LOC NINH III	18 Aug	1/2 Inf; 2d Sqd 11 Cav.	200	75 miles N. Saigon
LOC NINH IV	7 Sep	1/2 Inf; 2/16 Inf; 1/28 Inf; 11 Arm Cav; Div Arty.	216	75 miles N. Saigon
JULIE	26 Oct	2/28 Inf.	86	85 miles N. NW Saigon
	1 Nov	1/26 Inf; ¼ Cav; Div Arty.	27	15 miles NE Tay Ninh
	8-11 Nov	11 Arm Cav.	70	75 miles N. Saigon
JUNCTION CITY	1 Dec	2/28 Inf.	44	8 miles W. Lai Khe
	1 Dec	1/18 Inf; 11 Arm Cav.	43	5 miles E. Lai Khe

MAJOR BATTLES

NAME OF BATTLE	DATE	U.S. UNITS	ENEMY KILLED	LOCATION
	1967			
XOM BO I	14 Jun	B Co, 1/16 Inf; Div Arty.	60	35 miles N. NE Saigon
XOM BO II	17 Jun	Recon 1/16 Inf; A,B,C, Co 1/16 Inf; A,B Co 2/28 Inf; 2/33 Arty.	222	40 miles N. NE Saigon
DA YEU	6 Oct	B, C, D Co 1/18 Inf; A Co 1/5 Arty: ; B Co 2/33 Arty; B Co 6/15 Arty; 8/6 Arty.	59	45 miles N Saigon
ONG THANH	17 Oct	Recon, A, B, C, D 2/28 Inf; B, C 2/33 Arty; B Co 6/16 Arty; A Co 1/5 Arty; A Co 8/6 Arty; D Co 1/16 Inf.	163	12 miles NW Lai Khe
SROK SILAMLITE I	29 Oct	A, C, D Co 1/18 Inf; CIDG Co.	24	75 miles N Saigon
SROK SILAMITE II	30 Oct	A, D Co 1/18 Inf; CIDG Co; Bn CMD GP.	83	75 miles N Saigon
LOC NINH AIR STRIP	31 Oct	A Btry 6/15 Arty.	82	75 miles N Saigon
SROK SILAMLITE III	2 Nov	A, C, D 1/18 Inf; A Btry 2/33 Arty.	263	75 miles N Saigon
BU NHO RUNG	3 Nov	2/12 25 Div; Div Arty.	56	75 miles N Saigon
SROK RUNG	7 Nov	D, C Co 1/26 Inf; CMD Grp 1/26 Inf; A Bt ry 6/15 Arty; B Btry 2/33 Arty.	66	5 miles E. NE Loc Ninh
BU DOP	29-30 Nov	A Btry 2/33 Arty; 1/28 Inf (−)	31	90 miles N Saigon
HILL 172	8 Dec	1/2 Inf; B Btry 1/5 Arty; A Btry 2/33 Arty; ARVN 155 mm Btry.	49	2 miles SE Bu Dop
XA CAT	10 Dec	A Co 1/18 Inf; 3d Plt C Trp ½ Cav; A Btry 6/15 Arty; C Btry 8/6 Arty.	143	4 miles S. An Loc

MAJOR COMBAT OPERATIONS

1 MAY 67–31 DEC 68

NAME OF OPERATION	DATE	ENEMY KILLED	WEAPONS CAPTURED OR DESTROYED
MANHATTAN	23 Apr-11 May	123	417 small arms, 9 crew-served; 460,000 rounds small arms ammo; 5,331 mortar rounds; 26 rockets; 3,587 lb explosives; 186 CBU; 104 claymores, 327 mines, 2,083 grenades, 34 Bangalore torpedos; 626.38 tons rice, 5.65 tons wheat; 21.75 tons salt; medical supplies; 1 cow; 4.05 tons cement; 3 outboard motors; 187 sheets tin.
DALLAS	17 May-25 May	19	9 small arms, 1 crew-served; 20 mortar, 175 claymores, 12 mines; 15 cans soybean oil, 10 bottles vitamins, 1 dial telephone, 11 cats.
BILLINGS	12 June-26 Jun	347	1 chicom carbine, 2 AK 50's, 1 light machinegun; ammunition; mines, 2 pigs.
PAUL BUNYAN I	19 Jul-13 Aug	0	50 rounds small arms ammo; 65 artillery rounds; 5-500lb bombs; 2 cases dynamite; 1.4 tons rice.
PAUL BUNYAN II	16 Aug-11 Sep	3	2 small arms, 1 RPG, 87 grenades, 2-250 lb bombs, 5-500lb bombs; 1 pair sandals.
SHENANDOAH II	29 Sep-19 Nov	957	70 small arms, 31 crew-served, 3 flame throwers, 6,316 rounds small arms ammo, 174 mortar rounds, 134 rockets, 101 RPG rounds, 30 mines, 141 booby traps, 41 lb gun powder; 246.9 tons rice, 29 tons salt, 1,200 lb sugar, medical supplies, 1 sewing machine, 1 blackboard.
QUYET THANG	11 Mar-7 Apr	429 (BC) 246 (POSS)	119 small arms, 31 crew-served, 6.032 small arms ammo, 382 mortar rounds, 121 RPG rounds, 350 grenades, 77 anti-tank mines, 30 anti-personnel mines, 510 lb explosives, 1560 blasting caps; 64 tons rice, 4,896 lb salt, 450 lb sugar, 250 lb peas, 900 lb pork, 1775 lb eggs, 5,900 lb milk; 7,500 ft common wire, 51b soap.
TOAN THANG I	7 Apr-31 May	1739	362 individual weapons, 79 crew-served, 405 mortar rounds, 368 RPG rounds, 44,380 rounds small arms, 1.025 grenades, 103 anti-personnel mines, 91 anti-tank mines; 31 bicycles; 97 tons rice, 5 tons salt, 13 tons foodstuff; 71-122 rockets, 29-107 rockets.
TOAN THANG II	1 June-31 Jan 69	2,549	1438 individual weapons, 222 crew-served weapons, 315,034 small arms ammo, 5,219 anti-tank mines, 4,167 grenades, 1,858 anti-personnel mines, 2,536 RPG rounds, 4.283 mortar rounds; 474.6 tons rice, 38.9 tons foodstuffs; 1,069 lb explosives, 185 rockets.

Notes

1   "Basic Combat Training". United States Army. goarmy. com/soldier-life/becoming-a-soldier/basic-combat-train-ing.html

2   "Basic Combat Training". United States Army. goarmy. com/soldier-life/becoming-a-soldier/basic-combat-train-ing.html

3   US Army Joint Readiness Training Center (JRTC) and Fort Polk History https://home.army.mil/polk/index.php/about/history

4   "History of the Big Red One": *The First Infantry Div. In Vietnam Volume 2* (1967), 30-33, First Division Museum Colonel Robert R. McCormick Research Center Digital Collection: nmtvault.com.

5   *Danger Forward Volume 2, Issue 4* (December 1, 1968) First Division Museum Colonel Robert R. McCormick Research Center Digital Collection: Civic Action RRMRC Digital Collection: nmtvault.com.

6   Detroit Historical Society

7   'C-Rats' fueled troops during and after World War II. Aug. 13, 2019. David Vergun. https//www.defense.gov

8   *Danger Forward Volume 2, Issue 4* (December 1, 1968) First Division Museum Colonel Robert R. McCormick Research Center Digital Collection: Civic Action RRMRC Digital Collection: nmtvault.com.

9   *Danger Forward Volume 2, Issue 4* (December 1, 1968) First Division Museum Colonel Robert R. McCormick Research Center Digital Collection: Civic Action RRMRC Digital Collection: nmtvault.com.

10 History - US Marshals and the Pentagon Riot of 1967 https://usmarshals.gov/history/civilian/1967a.htm

11 The First Infantry Div. in Vietnam, Collection: 1st Infantry Div. Pub. - Vietnam RRMRC Digital Collection.

12 The First Infantry Div. in Vietnam, Collection: 1st Infantry Div. Pub. - Vietnam RRMRC Digital Collection.

13 *Danger Forward Volume 2, Issue 4* (December 1, 1968) First Division Museum Colonel Robert R. McCormick Research Center Digital Collection: Civic Action RRMRC Digital Collection: nmtvault.com.

14 *Danger Forward Volume 2, Issue 4* (December 1, 1968) First Division Museum Colonel Robert R. McCormick Research Center Digital Collection: Civic Action RRMRC Digital Collection: nmtvault.com.

15 *Danger Forward Volume 2, Issue 3* (September 1, 1968) First Division Museum Colonel Robert R. McCormick Research Center Digital Collection: nmtvault.com.

16 *Danger Forward Volume 2, Issue 4* (December 1, 1968) First Division Museum Colonel Robert R. McCormick Research Center Digital Collection: Civic Action RRMRC Digital Collection: nmtvault.com.

17 *Danger Forward Volume 2, Issue 4* (December 1, 1968) First Division Museum Colonel Robert R. McCormick Research Center Digital Collection: Civic Action RRMRC Digital Collection: nmtvault.com.

18 *Danger Forward Volume 2, Issue 4* (December 1, 1968) First Division Museum Colonel Robert R. McCormick Research Center Digital Collection: Civic Action RRMRC Digital Collection: nmtvault.com.

19 *Danger Forward Volume 2, Issue 3* (September 1, 1968) First Division Museum Colonel Robert R. McCormick Research Center Digital Collection: nmtvault.com.

20 *Danger Forward Volume 2, Issue 3* (September 1, 1968) First Division Museum Colonel Robert R. McCormick Research Center Digital Collection: nmtvault.com.

Photography Credits

All photographs courtesy of the First Division Museum Colonel Robert R. McCormick Research Center Digital Collection, unless noted below.

Pages 11, 30, 57, 66, 73, 193, 198, 199, 202-207, 230, 231, 233-241: Family of Jack Freppon

Page 23: Photographs taken by William Anemone, courtesy of the William Anemone Estate

Page 51: Detroit Historical Society

Page 70: Olson. K.R. and Morton, L.W. (2017). Why were the soil tunnels of Cu Chi and Iron Triangle in Vietnam so resilient? Open Journal of Soil Science, 7, 34-51. https//doi.org/10.4326/ojss.2017.72003

Page 96: *Internal Medicine in Vietnam, Volume I,* "Chapter 6: Skin Diseases in Vietnam 1965-72", Lieutenant Colonel Alfred M. Allen, MC, USA. U.S. Army Medical Department, Office of Medical History. https://history.amedd.army.mil/booksdocs/vietnam/skindiseases/chapter6.htm

CPSIA information can be obtained
at www.ICGtesting.com
Printed in the USA
FSHW010736290620
71621FS